THE END OF NATURAL SELECTION

www.ingramcontent.com/pod-product-compliance
Lightning Source LLC
Chambersburg PA
CBHW020001290326
41935CB00007B/266

THE END OF NATURAL SELECTION

SIMON LENNON

Pine Hill Books

The End of Natural Selection

Non-fiction

Demography, Workplace Culture

A book in the collection: The West

A book in the series: Individualism

Published by Pine Hill Books

Copyright © 2016, © 2020 by Simon Lennon

ISBN 978-1-925446-09-8 (electronic)

ISBN 978-1-925446-12-8 (paperback)

55,000 words, plus bibliography to 56,000 words

Cover image: The annual finance division conference of Cement Australia, 2005

To my descendants, not yet born

Contents

1

Unnatural Selection

Through one early revision of this writing, I found myself setting threshold, budget, and stretch numbers of chapters to revise in a day. Cement Australia set such numbers for profit, injury rates, and I imagine much more, taking the lead from its Australian American shareholder. Driving performance endlessly upward, they were a means of measuring monetary bonuses. No longer using economies to improve Western lives, Western lives had become means of improving economies.

Increasingly since the Second World War, we have become the unnatural West. What I call unnatural selection is people picking who'll prosper (materially, at any rate, if only for a while) and who else will procreate, when we do so with our natures corrupted, desires unnatural, and instincts denied.

Natural selection is different. It's natural. Without Western individualism but with their innate tribal instincts intact, other races prefer *their* people prosper and procreate, linking the two.

Englishman Charles Darwin and his 1859 book *On the Origin of Species* were sufficiently influential and still sufficiently well known, at least to museum curators and visitors, to form an exhibition of his life and work at the Australian National Museum in the summer of 2009. (Admittedly, my three eldest children were less interested than I was to inspect it.) Darwin's book introduced the world to his theories of natural selection, which he'd developed through decades and about which he'd been writing and talking for years beforehand (giving me great comfort with my writing).

"*As many more individuals of each species are born than can possibly survive,*" Darwin wrote in the book's introduction, "*and as, consequently, there is a frequently recurring struggle for existence, it follows that any being, if it vary however slightly in any manner profitable to itself, under the complex and sometimes varying conditions of life, will have a better chance of surviving, and thus be naturally selected. From the strong principle of inheritance, any selected variety will tend to propagate its new and modified form.*" Thus the species over generations evolves.

That book didn't explicitly include human beings among the life forms that Darwin theorised enjoyed natural selection. His 1871 book *The Descent of Man, and Selection in Relation to Sex* did: human evolution. We think most about Darwin's theory that human beings and apes share common ancestors, but natural selection doesn't depend on it. Human beings might have always been human beings distinct from apes, but still over generations evolve.

After reading Darwin's first book, British philosopher Herbert Spencer wrote *Principles of Biology* published in 1864, linking his economic with Darwin's biological theories. "*This survival of the fittest,*" wrote Spencer, "*which I have here sought to express in mechanical terms, is that which Mr. Darwin has called 'natural selection', or the preservation of favoured races in the struggle for life.*"

Darwin liked Spencer's phrase. In *The Variation of Animals and Plants under Domestication* published in 1868, he wrote, "*This preservation, during the battle for life, of varieties which possess any advantage in structure, constitution, or instinct, I have called Natural Selection; and Mr. Herbert Spencer has well expressed the same idea by the Survival of the Fittest. The term "natural selection" is in some respects a bad one, as it seems to imply conscious choice; but this will be disregarded after a little familiarity.*"

Being the fittest and thus being naturally selected isn't necessarily a matter of being physically or mentally superior. It's a matter of fitting in best with the immediate environment. Living in the open air, a person does well to be tall. Living in caves, a person does well to be short.

By the early twenty-first century, natural selection was over. "If you want to know what Utopia is like, just look around – this is it," said Welsh geneticist Steve Jones of University College London in 2002. "Things have simply stopped getting better, or worse, for our species."

The air is neither hot nor cold inside centrally conditioned buildings. No sounds, dampness, nor changes in temperature break through. Working at office desks with double-glazed windows behind me, I could turn and discover a previously blue sky had become a raging, dark storm. Amidst the rampant abundance of amenities and technologies, the scrawny no longer fall sick and die. They collect their medicines over the counter. The stupid take, or miss, extra classes.

We in the West have done something more. Our postmodern West isn't natural. It's ideological: a peculiar political and economic environment. Few conditions of life have been more complex or varied, whether we notice or not. Natural selection is premised upon differences, but we insist upon everyone being equal. It's premised upon inclusion of some and exclusion of others, but we insist upon inclusion of all: trying to ensure everyone fits in. We reject natural selection for being discriminatory.

Indifferent to human evolution, we're more likely to favour other races than our own, provided we personally survive. If there's to be evolution within our race, it will be moneyed evolution. Those with a better chance of surviving are those that vary however slightly in a manner profitable to buyers and employers while remaining acceptable to our ideological keepers, rather than anything physical or intellectual. Survival of the fittest means survival of the richest.

By the time I arrived at Cement Australia in September 2003, forty-one years of age, I knew to work and watch, study and see. Cement made the companies for which I'd previously worked seem like evolutionary steps along our new Western way. TNT Limited and its subsidiary TNT Shipping & Development Limited, Holyman Limited, and Otter Gold Mines Limited had initially been good places to work. They each changed during my time there (and not, I trust, because I worked there). Each successive change came sooner.

Like the climactic moments of a television quiz show, the shimmering curtains drew open to reveal the glistening main prize: Cement. I saw, sat with, and listened to the people the West was becoming, in all our skill and conviction, our pride and our glitz. Slowly I realised, we'd already met.

In 1989, after I'd suffered several throat infections, a surgeon diagnosed my lower jaw as not sitting and pivoting properly in my upper jaw. As I discovered later, corrective surgery would mean that, for the first time in my life, I would be able to bite neatly on a sandwich: my private Utopia. In our Western democracies championing choice and individual rights, the surgeon would only operate on my jaw after I bought private health insurance. I did, twelve months before he could operate. I've renewed it ever since.

Of itself, the surgeon's action could have been perfectly natural, but earning the income to buy health insurance (along with food, clothing, and shelter) makes our prosperity not so much a matter of nature as a matter of money. People without governments, families, or other benefactors to keep them need jobs. In my second last year of school, I realised I could only ever live in a nice house by earning the income to buy it; nobody was going to buy it for me or give it to me. I thus studied hard, becoming a lawyer.

Natural selection rewards individuals and species. Unnatural selection rewards only individuals.

Darwin's theory of natural selection set out the theories he developed from observing the natural world through his five-year voyage a passenger aboard His Majesty's Ship *Beagle*, beginning in 1831. Instead of a ship carrying me, I made my observations in law firms and companies, particularly from 1987. Where I wasn't a participant, I was a traveller passing through. Darwin paid, or his family paid, his fare. I received salaries and other payments of money. Instead of birds, plants, insects, and animals to observe, I observed people. The distinction with animals wasn't quite what it needed to be.

University educated as he was, Darwin was essentially an amateur in the field about which he wrote, beyond some academic success collecting beetles. I'm much the same, without the beetles.

Much of the selection we individuals make is by our indifference to others. Employers employ for themselves. Employees work for themselves. (When employees become unemployed, we're nothing at all.) Earning income depends upon decisions by self-interested sellers and employers. Vendors want customers. Customers want service. Once in a while, their interests coincide.

Paying the most money, corporations are the most influential employers, pervasive marketers, and prolific buyers and sellers in markets of purchase and sale, but corporations don't really exist. They're legal fictions we created to carry on commerce. All that exist are people behind the wide veils: directors, executives, managers, and employees, even lawyers, normally hidden from view. Corporations are secret societies, about which people outside know little. Admission is by invitation only.

No business allows people to enter its premises as freely as we once allowed neighbours into our homes. Without a receptionist at her desk and sometimes with one, toughened-glass doors to offices are locked fast. Cleaning contractors early evenings and employees all the time carry keys or security cards we slip through sensory grooves by the doors, admitting us. Images around company walls focus on company business, instructing and even inspiring employees and visitors (although not, I suspect, cleaning contractors).

I offer exposés of Western company cultures, for want of a better term (and thus Western cultures, for want of a better term), for people who've not experienced them and, I trust, new perspectives for people who have. Some readers will see my writing as dire warnings about what we're doing to each other and ourselves. Others will see it as modules of a confidential corporate training manual. Others will just wait for the jokes, hoping there's one in every paragraph. Sorry.

Corporate selection we call recruitment. The recruitment consultant who interviewed me late in 2002 saw I was eager to leave my novels behind. After all, I spent the interview leaning forward across the table towards her. The truth would've cost me my chance that she'd recommend me for a job. I wanted money.

People living in comfortable homes aren't so brave to weather those not so nice, let alone go back with five children to the home unit where we'd lived with one child or enter a caravan park. Well-to-do white people don't want to be the first person we know receiving payments of welfare. (Being the second, third, or fiftieth person is fine.) To be certain we could remain well fed and clothed in our nice home forever, while I wrote novels nobody published, I needed to repay my debts.

Two century-old companies, one pre-eminent in south-eastern Australia and the other in north-eastern Australia, merged to form Cement Australia in May 2003. Together, its plants produced almost fifty percent of all that Australia produced of its principal product: cement, funnily enough. Half owned by a Swiss company, Cement sold more than two thirds of its cement to its other two shareholders: the Australian subsidiary of an English company and an Australian American company. With plants, mines, and ships in place and so many sales secure, it couldn't help but make money: a great deal of money.

While interviewing me with the inaugural chief financial officer Gary, the inaugural human resources manager Paul feared I'd be bored at Cement after my work at Holyman. I convinced him he was wrong, that I was surprised he imagined such a thing. Ironically as everything turned out, being bored was a luxury I would rarely enjoy.

Only acting in the role, Paul had been willing to join Cement's head office in Sydney in a capacity other than human resources. Chris, the new chief executive, refused him. Paul found an operational role with the Swiss shareholder in America but had he remained at Cement, I might never have written this book.

Natural selection hasn't ended altogether. In 2013, Aarhus University political scientist Michael Petersen and other academics reported the results of their studies of men and women in America, Argentina, and Denmark, finding that strong men are more likely to support economic self-reliance. Weak men are more likely to support the welfare state and economic redistribution. (They found no correlations among women.)

In the West, the weak prevail, but we're not redistributing wealth to the physically weak and intellectually strong. That would be discriminatory. We're simply redistributing it.

Wayne, the new Cement human resources general manager, once remarked in a conversation between us that short men and ugly women find jobs harder to come by. Wayne was among the tallest people with whom I worked, physically strong I'd have thought. I don't think he was calling me short.

"My research shows being good-looking helps you earn more money, find a higher-earning spouse, and even get better deals on mortgages," said American economist Daniel Hamermesh in 2011. "Some people are born ugly, and there's not much they can do about it."

Whenever natural selection pops up, the West now tries to eradicate it. Equating ugliness to race and disability, discrimination against ugly people became lookism. American woman Shirley Ivey, sixty-one years old, sued her former employer after resigning from her job, because she'd recently put on weight and her supervisor told her he would like her more if she were prettier.

People don't become equal because we now think they are. As much deliberately as by our indifference, we're driving the human species down.

By 2012, people were becoming dumber, according to Stanford University geneticist Gerald Crabtree. "*I would wager that if an average citizen from Athens of 1000 BC were to appear suddenly among us, he or she would be among the brightest and most intellectually alive of our colleagues and companions, with a good memory, a broad range of ideas, and a clear-sighted view of important issues,*" he wrote. "*Furthermore, I would guess that he or she would be among the most emotionally stable of our friends and colleagues.*"

Crabtree attributed it to adverse genetic mutations that natural selection no longer weeded out, but they mightn't be the only forces at work. (Our education systems aren't helping.) Other studies have linked diminishing intelligence with consuming fluoride in the water supply, pesticides used in food production, processed foods, and high-fructose corn syrup.

Human devolution doesn't bother the West. We're not so judgemental.

Central to our Western ideologies of equality is our individualism. In

2013, drawing upon the work of mathematician John Nash, Michigan State University biologists Christoph Adami and Arend Hintze published research suggesting evolution favours those who co-operate over those who don't. Any benefit from acting alone is short-lived, because others soon adapt their strategies accordingly.

"Darwin himself was puzzled about the co-operation you observe in nature," commented Leicester University psychologist Andrew Colman. "He was particularly struck by social insects. You might think that natural selection should favour individuals that are exploitative and selfish, but in fact we now know after decades of research that this is an oversimplified view of things…"

Evolution favours nationalism and other tribalism over individualism. The West persists with individualism.

2

Relationship and Parenthood

The people most surprised by Cement Australia were my parents-in-law, whose working lives had ended soon after mine was getting under way. They'd come from a time of community, kindness, and contentment. Men stood up for women, we all stood up for pregnant women. Most proudly, my mother-in-law would've called herself a homemaker, my father-in-law a family man; a common compliment was to call a man a good family man.

Employers preferred to employ married people with children for being more complete, stable, and grounded. We saw people with dependants, particularly children, to support as being more deserving of the privilege of income, often paying them more money than we paid bachelors. Thinking in terms of our nations and races, their children were our children: our futures. Those times might return to the West but, for the moment, they've passed.

In the rush of their jobs and business balance sheets, some company executives might feel differently in calm moments away from the office or heat of a meeting. I hope so. The closer the walls around people seated together, the stronger the pressures the group exert on each individual, the greater the compulsion to conform.

Before I'd joined the first law firm at which I worked after my Supreme Court admission in 1986, an insurance partner became romantically involved with a solicitor. Frank and Audrey had everything to share: their work. He championed her promotion to senior associate of the firm, while their relationship grew to marriage and children. They later separated.

What once we'd encouraged, we banned. The firm prohibited staff becoming romantically involved together; nothing as personal as love should again affect promotions, dismissals, or anything else about work. Spiro and Litsa kept their relationship secret; they each departed.

Even less than we want the complications of other people's relationships, do we want complications of ours. A senior associate litigation lawyer quietly walked every afternoon from the offices, returning an hour or so later. Nobody knew where Malcolm went, although rumour was that the bachelor living with his mother frequented a brothel. Paying not just for friends, some pay for lovers.

A colleague at a law firm at which I worked in 1988 (and a student from the year ahead of me at school), Richard M refused to become romantically involved with any of his colleagues. "A bird never sh*ts in his own nest," he explained.

Companies feared suits for harassment if one employee propositioned another although, as Wayne pointed out at Cement, the propositions needed to be repeated and unwelcome to constitute harassment. I never heard of Wayne making or for that matter receiving propositions. Neither did I, at Cement.

Relating well with potential managers and colleagues remained a condition of securing a job or promotion. After interviewing (with the chief executive and chief financial officer) each of the three shortlisted candidates for the legal general manager role at Otter Gold Mines in 2000, the human resources manageress Ros asked the receptionist how we'd each acted waiting to be led from the reception area into the boardroom. Ros like that I'd chatted with the receptionist, although our conversation was about nothing in particular. I knew conversation could only assist me.

I can't imagine anyone three years later at Cement taking an interest in my conversations with the receptionist Dragana (gentler than her name suggested), while awaiting my interviews. We still choose candidates with whom we feel comfortable, but so individualistic have we become, we aren't looking to become close to our colleagues.

A decade earlier, during my studies for a Master of Business Administration degree, my managerial psychology lecturer taught us how to pass the multiple-choice personality tests many prospective employers required. We should choose the middle positions on everything. We should love our parents, but our mothers a little more than our fathers.

Employers are no longer looking for sane, emotionally balanced employees. More sophisticated in the choices it made, Cement subjected the final three candidates for the company secretary role to half a day of exhaustive psychological and other tests. Among many, many other things, my replies included saying that people's personal problems shouldn't affect other people's expectations of their work. We appoint team-minded individuals eager to learn, work, and earn, from whom we remain comfortably apart. (The two unsuccessful candidates might've been nicer people than I was.)

A logical and illogical consequence of our new Western individualism is to separate prosperity from procreation, at least among us. The man I call Griff endorsed the head of Holyman Limited's Danish subsidiary refusing to hire a woman he thought might become pregnant, flagrantly flouting Danish law. Secretly that night, from the telephone in my home unit, I contacted a lawyer in Denmark. Jacob would ensure the Danish manager understood his legal obligations.

Subverting my chief executive might've been unethical (ethicists can debate that one to and fro), but I didn't care. I was being moral. I couldn't change the thoughts in the Danish manager's head or force him to comply with the spirit Danish laws intended, but I could bring some small pressure upon him. Rejecting corporatism as much as individualism, I cared about Danes enough to care about a woman I didn't know and the family she'd not yet grown.

We're creating model employees, but in just one or two generations, my family has become rare. My wife credited the conception of our fifth child so soon after the birth of our fourth with me being unemployed at the time. I was thus able to contribute more to parenting our children already born, although not at the point of our fifth child's conception.

The converse to our fifth was our sixth and final child, conceived in the confidence when Cement was a good place to work. Not that conception occurred at the office.

Linda Wayman, the head of Southern Cross Austereo in Perth and a mother of two, told the Mumbrella Perth Conference in 2015 that she kept a "big jar of condoms at work," trying to keep her staff from bearing babies. She didn't believe women returning from maternity leave should automatically be able to work part-time, calling it "an idealistic and anti-commercial stance."

Like natural selection before it, unnatural selection can be cruel. In 2012, Sydney University vice chancellor Michael Spence told me of research at the University of Queensland suggesting young men are more likely than young women to speak of wanting marriage and children, because young women feel pressured to want a career.

We want people to find satisfaction from careers, competing with other people's careers. We become what we want others to be.

We regard it as perfectly proper to carry out school programmes and advertising campaigns encouraging people to work, enter trades, or take apprenticeships. Encouraging them to join the armed forces can be a little controversial. They can do whatever they want to do, provided they want careers.

University of Texas, San Antonio researcher Kristina Durante and others in 2012 suggested women may be choosing careers because they feel suitable, appealing, and available men are too few. Much like natural selection, women who feel they're least likely to secure a mate are more likely to choose career, to avoid the disappointment of wanting marriage but failing. (They might feel, rightly or wrongly, they're unattractive to men, but it's a rare woman who's not beautiful when she smiles.)

Men might no longer be sufficiently financially resourced to appeal to women. Men and women might be lulled into wanting something else. The risk of divorce might frighten them from marriage altogether.

Natural selection promotes procreation. Unnatural selection doesn't, not among us. There's not enough profit; not soon enough anyway. We exhort working and spending, rather than motherhood and fatherhood. Unnatural selection promotes everything but parenthood. We've the money to do so.

It's hard to imagine anyone but white people being like the young American woman whose words were part of a lecture during my Business studies; I think the subject was cross-cultural management in 1995. Determined only to do what she could do well, she said she could either be a good mother or do her job well, but not both. So, she wasn't going to be a mother at all.

Too many of us do just what we feel: forsaking feelings for which we're unprepared. That so many in the West don't feel the desire to be parents speaks less of the desire than it speaks about us.

The times of my life when each of my children was born surpassed all others, but neither my wife nor I having realised our innate human instincts qualifies me to write this book. My qualification comes from the time before I came to be so fortunate to have all I have now: as much from my time of ignorance as experience.

A decade or so older than I was, Peter B studied at the London School of Economics. He went onto receive a Master of Business Administration degree from the University of Chicago. A business manager at TNT Shipping & Development, his office on the floor above mine featured a product of his keen interest in photography: a picture of a huge gorilla he'd seen in Rwanda during a five-week African holiday.

Peter's responsibilities included managing the construction of a monorail system. At a meeting to discuss a financially disastrous café under a monorail station, Peter agreed to release four Egyptian tenants from the lease they'd signed. "How could I do anything else?" he asked me afterwards, after one of the Egyptians arrived appearing heavily pregnant. The State Bank of New South Wales also released them from their debts, although none of us really knew the money they had. Maximising profit didn't diminish our trust or generosity.

Several people in that company were kind, but perhaps Peter's indulgence had a particular impetus. In the first week of October 1992, we shared five days together in the Northern Territory to settle the terms of a contract appointing another company to manage TNT's gas pipeline. Before the trip, Peter asked me if I could stay in the Territory an extra day, until Saturday. I said I could, assuming he was about to tell me we'd have a meeting that Friday in Darwin. He didn't. He said we'd been invited to go barramundi fishing in Kakadu.

With more than enough time for us to talk in airline lounges, hotels, and restaurants that week, none of our conversations I would recall so many years afterward as I recalled one during the balmy early Wednesday evening at the Wharf restaurant near Darwin. Peter told me he'd married his wife, a fitness instructor, instead of merely living with her because she wanted children. He'd never cared one way or the other about becoming a father but, when their son Sebastian was born, he held the newborn baby in his arms. Completely besotted, Peter stared endlessly at him. Being a father was the greatest thing that ever happened to him.

I'd also studied well and, in time, would earn a Master of Business Administration degree. I'd also travelled and would travel more. I believed Peter for what he said about him and his life, but I'm not sure I believed what was true for him would also be true for me. I should've.

Most of TNT Shipping & Development became Holyman, without Peter B or the monorail but with the gas pipeline. (Never again did I visit Darwin or Kakadu.) Late one weekday night through the winter of 1995, at ten o'clock or so, I parked my car in Castlereagh Street, Sydney. Martin Place, so busy in daylight, was almost empty, while I sat among several of us in our suits through a telephone conference in a meeting room at the Minter Ellison law offices, discussing financing a ferry to operate in Denmark. By the time we walked from the building at around two o'clock in the morning, we might've been the only people there. I hope we were.

Stepping into my car with only the time for company, the dashboard clock shone in my dark, single space. The sense of my pregnant wife asleep at home struck me. With no greater duress than tiredness and the issues of work resolved as well as they could be, I didn't need relief, but still a wave of comfort and contentment swept through my business-suited body. I was overwhelmingly glad so soon to have a family to which I could go home each night or early morning.

Instead of corrupting human beings to suit economies, we could found economies upon human beings. The concept might seem radical, even ridiculous, but the West didn't think so during my parents-in-law's working lives. Other races still don't.

3

Physical Features

Before I joined TNT Shipping & Development in 1988, the company appointed advertising consultants to help market its monorail. The deepest impression those men made upon the company secretary Reuben was arriving at meetings with beautiful women at each arm. The women never said anything.

Reuben and the managing director Roly judged work by its quality, not the worker. Most managers then did. It all seems long ago.

Finding new extents of individualism since the West dispensed with race, we've gone onto dispense with discrimination after discrimination. Height, strength, and physical appearance became immoral, and sometimes illegal, discriminations because of their correlations with race. Even police forces relaxed their requirements, favouring racial and gender equality over safety and law enforcement. Soon enough, we'd removed from our thinking the physical features so fundamental to natural selection.

What used to be called handicaps came to be called disabilities, because they're not supposed to handicap people. Had TNT carried out formal performance appraisals, there'd have been no references to the shipping agency general manager's withered arm, hanging lifelessly from his slightly arched shoulder. Nobody mentioned it near him any more than a shopkeeper would mention it seeing him enter a store, although his secretary (and alleged mistress) might've mentioned it, in contexts not easily imaginable.

Disabilities disappear, except in dedicated parking spaces and seats on buses and trains, unless they inescapably affect a job's inherent requirements. We can be able-bodied or not, blind or able to see.

Bus drivers still need the power of sight, as was obvious to that motorist parked on Elizabeth Street when a bus in which I was a passenger in 1988 swiped off his car's side mirror. The motorist left his car, raced after the bus slowed in heavy traffic, and pounded his fist against the bus passenger door. The bus driver claimed ignorance of the broken mirror. (I can't think of any job more stressful for so little remuneration than being a bus driver.)

Train drivers have two tracks to guide them. Being able to see is a little less of an issue.

A very neat expression of how far we've gone in dispensing with people's physical characteristics was advice I received late in 2010 about my manuscript I now call *Western Individualism*. An assessor objected to me mentioning, in brackets, that Pauline was "*a Sri Lankan aged in her forties, or more.*" The assessor wrote that "*it remains unclear as to why this factor is important to either Pauline's role as a personal assistant, or germane to the unfolding story…*" Readers were to picture Pauline without thought of her race or age.

At every company for which I've worked, the managing director's personal assistant was also de facto or *de jure* office manageress. The assessor objected to my description of the office manageress at TNT Shipping & Development, Ann. "*Where's the value in his observation, for example, that…'If she wasn't middle-aged it was because she was older than that'?*" Having become middle-aged too, it was hardly an insult.

Removing physical descriptions and the contexts in which they appear makes our writing less informative, personal, and interesting, but that isn't the point. The assessor called irrelevant my observation: "*There were a surprisingly large number of short men among the senior-most business figures with whom I worked.*" We're supposed to wipe physical features from our words and minds.

That manuscript assessor nevertheless wanted "*a 360° perspective*" about characters. Whatever that meant, it didn't mean their heights, races, ages, weights, or anything else bodily about them, not in the West. It was a perspective outside a person, not of the person.

The most we envisage are descriptors like hairstyles and beards, which can be easily changed. We've disallowed the size of somebody's belly, more difficult to change. So the Fat Controller in the Reverend Awdry's stories of Thomas the Tank Engine became Sir Topham Hatt. My children made me conscious of that one.

We're not superficial in our physical evaluations of people. We're not evaluating them at all.

Our near-neighbour Kerry was the last person left in our street walking her dog and chatting with people. Around about 2011, she explained very well why we work so hard controlling our language. (Well, some parts of our language, anyway.) "When you have to think before you speak, it makes you think," she said. "If you have to choose your words, then it changes the way you think."

She meant so well, thinking about people with disabilities, but we apply the device to so much. We're manipulating our minds to particular points of view, and to having no view at all.

Human evolution doesn't depend upon individual evolution: individuals evolving within our lifetimes. It depends upon which people become parents, but our postmodern Western perspective avoids reference to people being parents or not. The assessor objected to me referring to what she called Ann's "*reproductive status, capacity, or sexual appearance.*"

By our postmodern measures, Ann had succeeded in her corporate career. "*The only woman wearing enough pale powder on her face for it to be obvious was Ann,*" I'd written. I suppose I'd seen the irony of her ensuring that secretaries wore dresses when I went onto say that "*nobody but Ann cared what she wore. That was aside from the days we sat with her at lunch and she wore blouses exposing her suddenly obvious and lilywhite cleavage. There was her skin without powder, and they were the only times she ever seemed quite maternal.*"

We're not to speak of maternity. "*Dominating Ann's desk was a photograph of her beloved husband, who surely wasn't so adored by women as she said he was. She also claimed he was a clever, skilled businessman. Ann mothered him but they were otherwise childless, although she complained bitterly to a group of young secretaries about a woman working upstairs, in the TNT head office. 'Women who have children and put them in childcare shouldn't have children,' she told them.*"

Completely unmentionable was anything about breastfeeding. "*At her age, her lilywhite cleavage was unlikely ever to be suckled as God had intended.*"

All those words, I deleted. At this time of our history, I was wrong to mention such matters. I'd been wrong to notice them.

Disabilities had become characteristics. Characteristics don't matter. They're a fact without judgement so the notion of treating them became disrespectful, although they might mean a person has special needs. (No longer is being average an insult and being special a compliment.) There are no congenital deformities, because there are no deformities.

In 2002, two deaf American lesbians, Sharon Duchesneau and Candy McCullough, chose a deaf sperm donor so their second child would be deaf. The first child he'd fathered for them was deaf.

We might strive to better our economic work and commercial product, but not people. That would reek of natural selection.

At least Duchesneau and McCullough bore children. In 2013, able-bodied British lesbian Chloe Jennings-White liked being in a wheelchair. She wanted an operation to paralyse her.

We can be of any physical form we want, especially in matters of vanity. Not merely curing us when we want to be cured, patients want cosmetic doctors to tailor our faces with lies and bodies with worse. The elder of my two sisters is on her third (or more) nose.

Companies declared employees their most valuable assets, perceiving people to be business resources: factors in the processes of production and consumption, cogs in other people's economies. Human resources departments came to call employees "human capital," akin to financial and physical capital. Whatever words we use to speak about others, people don't like being called human capital. He'd prefer "Hugh." She'd prefer "Minnie."

Words are economic tools no less than political ones. The most prolific exception to our proud ignorance about people's physical characteristics is when we laud differences between them: heterogeneity. When we draw upon all the people of the world to further our economic, ideological, and other individual self-interests, we call it diversity. We want everyone at work.

Nobody I've encountered lauded diversity more than Wayne's burgeoning human resources department at Cement Australia. Those physical traits and conditions otherwise lost from view were shouted from executive tables. Articles headed 'Diversity in Action' became commonplace in the company magazine. Long hands and bright camera lenses pointed gleefully at every new kind in the zoo. Instead of having no physical traits, employees conspicuously had all of them. The company magazine boasted the appointments of racial minorities, women, old people, young people, and a man with one arm (albeit healthy).

There hadn't been much physical diversity at the preceding three companies at which I worked as a corporate lawyer. Where there happened to be any, it was an outcome without having been an objective.

While physical discrimination became wrong, we increasingly discriminated according to people's economic usefulness to individual us. In 2008, the manager of an information technology company in Buesum, Germany, dismissed any of his ten employees who didn't smoke tobacco for disrupting the workplace.

Companies such as Otter and Cement required medical examinations of new employees, whatever their disabilities. Good health (disabilities notwithstanding) could thus have remained intrinsic to the human condition, to survival in our new Western world, except that employee health means just enough to work. The threshold of good health is low.

Continuing good health became a matter of company compliance. Otter provided influenza vaccinations each winter, so the chief executive decreed that any employees refusing to take them who later contracted the 'flu couldn't take sick leave. Such employees absent from work would surrender holiday leave. The legality of what Pat said didn't matter; it was never put to the test.

Cement monitored and managed employees' sick leave, which meant minimising it. With more pragmatism than compassion, managers sent home anyone carrying communicable diseases that could affect other employees' productivity, assigning them work they could undertake in quarantine. (Few people annoy me more than those employees stoically coming to work when they're sick, infecting the rest of us.) If an employee was malingering or fundamentally unwell, he or she was managed away. The company weeded out the unhealthy.

Merely being unwell is no reason for absence from work. The second manufacturing general manager continued working at Cement with a collapsed retina. Andre couldn't travel by aeroplane or otherwise enter high altitudes, but could work at his desk. (Wearing suits and working in offices can still be hard labour.)

If drugs can treat afflictions or their symptoms enough to keep someone working, then he or she remains able-bodied. Coal powered Cement's furnaces, and a coal miner injured in a gyrocopter accident (unrelated to his work at Cement) worked in the administrative office until he could again mine. Some sick days can be better than healthy days, with the right anaesthetics.

Many years have passed since I last had a sick day. I just switched on my computer and worked from home, as much as necessity demanded.

Cement formalised its incentives for employees to keep working by making injury rates across the company or the part of the company in which an employee worked determine as much as thirty percent of an executive or employee's annual bonus. Chewing on a white Mintie from the scores of lollies filling a glass bowl on the head office reception desk, I broke my tooth. Shaun (the inaugural sales and marketing general manager) dissuaded me from reporting it as an injury. "That would be a career-limiting move," he said.

The costs of repairing my tooth were infinitesimal to the company's annual profit, more than a hundred million dollars, even if the workers compensation insurer hadn't paid them. I never reported the injury, paid the dental costs myself, and didn't eat another Mintie for years.

Within the caverns of production and supply, employees are neither managed nor led. They're punished or rewarded. Few managers inspire respect or devotion; few even try. We don't always assert what we want, if we know assertion would affect our jobs, remuneration, or promotions in ways we don't want. (Sometimes, we get it wrong.)

The glass bowl soon also contained chocolate toffee Fantales. Chewing on one, I again broke a tooth. Without needing to consult Shaun, I never formally reported the injury and again paid my dental costs, although I mentioned what happened to my colleagues. The glass bowl soon vanished. In the interests of good health, Wayne would later instruct head office (and the Brisbane office) to provide trays of fresh fruit each week.

Unnatural selection doesn't end the struggle to survive. The struggle is simply in unnatural environments.

Once heading into a lift at Holyman, the development manager Ian Biner and I described the doctors in whom we had confidence. To paraphrase, I didn't want a doctor with no concept of tax-effective cross-border financial restructuring. Ian didn't want one who didn't even know where the Cayman Islands (well renowned for tax avoidance, money laundering, and business secrecy) were.

If employees were injured at Cement, the company required the responsible managers to take them to a company-approved doctor or hospital. They were doctors who wouldn't exempt sick and injured employees from work altogether, but only from work they were unfit to perform.

Employees didn't recuperate at home if they could recuperate in a company workplace performing proverbial light duties, which occupational health and safety laws allowed, even expected, employers to find. Employees continued working for as long as they could still use a telephone or computer even if their spleens hung from their bellies, provided not too much blood spilt on the floor.

4

The End of Excellence

In 1988, while searching newspapers for my first job outside a law firm, I came across an advertisement listing several aspects of people the New South Wales government (an equal opportunity employer) disregarded when hiring them to design and build bridges. I confess to being a little unsettled when I read mental illness among them. I should've been more unsettled when next I drove over a bridge.

Too often I hear people say the West has replaced aristocracy with meritocracy. We've done no such thing.

We aren't people of excellence. In the contest between excellence and diversity, we want diversity. In 2011, the American Department of Justice required the Dayton Police Department, Ohio, to lower its testing standards for recruits because not enough African Americans passed the examination. New York City Public School PS139 ceased its gifted student programme, Students of Academic Rigor, in 2014 because the classes were so much whiter than the student body overall.

In 2019, the West Midlands Fire Service recruitment programme required white male applicants to score seven out of ten in a verbal and numerical reasoning test. It required women and people from ethnic minorities to score only six out of ten. It wanted at least sixty percent of new recruits to be women and at least thirty-five percent to be from ethnic minorities by 2021.

"West Midlands Fire Service is committed to having a workforce which reflects the diversity of the population of all our communities, and one that is welcoming to all," said a spokesman. "We are working hard to break down barriers faced by people who could bring so much to our service and to their community."

The service was not so welcoming of white men. Those barriers to ethnic minorities were their inferior verbal and numerical reasoning abilities.

Excellence is exclusionary. Excellence is also racist.

During the first semester in San Diego in 2019, only seven percent of failing grades went to white students. Twenty-three percent went to each of Native Americans and Hispanics and twenty percent went to black students. Trying to erase those disparities in its opposition to racism, the San Diego Unified School District responded by removing consideration of punctuality in handing in work and consideration of behaviour.

There was also concern that the school district's zero-tolerance of cheating was unfair upon non-white students, presumably because they were more likely to cheat. That policy was under review.

We're inclusive no matter how naughty or stupid people are. We prefer equality to quality.

The 2004 American animated film *The Incredibles* neatly encapsulated our new Western attitudes to strengths, skills, and talent. Bob was incredibly strong, resistant to harm, and had enhanced sensory perceptions, but couldn't reveal any of his superhuman abilities in his job, sitting at a desk squeezed in a cubicle among scores of identical desks and cubicles. The Insuricare insurance company wanted him to reject customer claims on the basis of legal and contractual technicalities.

Helen pleaded with her young son Dash not to run as fast as he could, but instead to run only as fast as everyone else: to be like everyone else. She told him that everyone was special, as we in the West like to think, but her son knew that everyone being special was tantamount to no one being special.

We want everyone equal. Equality requires mediocrity.

Quality costs profit and revenue. When I studied at the University of New South Wales from 1988 to 1990, the Faculty of Commerce expelled Master of Commerce students if we failed any subject. It later dropped that condition.

Educational authorities want students to pass, so they'll re-enrol next year. "In order to deal with the students who were being recruited," said researcher Bob Birrell of the foreign students paying fees to Monash University, Melbourne in 2010, "they had to dumb down the curriculum."

A report by the Victorian Ombudsman revealed that, several days before the aerospace examination, a teacher handed out the examination paper to a Middle Eastern student, who then shared it with other Middle Eastern students. Telephone records of the teacher and several students showed conversations late at night in the days before a test on the stress on aeroplane components.

We achieve equality as we always do: by reducing the good until everything's as bad as the worst. Whenever all things become equal, they become the least. We prefer people to be equally stupid than suffer the ignominy of anyone being cleverer than anyone else.

Without a culture of quality or discrimination, everything's a commodity of one form or another, including people. We're commoditised according to work: lawyers and so forth. Provided we achieve an acceptable threshold of ability, all those within a category are pretty much alike. We're like barley, wheat, and other grains, little pieces of silver buried in constructing toast racks, and lead pencils. There are no matters of merit, but only of price.

Our only other distinguishing features are values and character. We hire belligerent lawyers, as long as they're not belligerent with us.

While I studied Science/Law at university, Malcolm studied Commerce/Law. We'd not seen each other for years when we saw each other again at his father's funeral. More than twenty years in the workforce, he didn't credit his becoming a law firm partner with his intellect. "People," he told me, referring as much to clients as the partners who'd appointed him, "realised I was going to beat down doors for them."

Within each corporation is a plethora of more secret societies, never letting the people within get close and never trusting the people without. Normally concentric and ever shrinking in size, eventually they hone in on directors. Even people inside corporations know little about them.

Company seniority has little to do with ability (as people working near executives would attest), physical prowess, or beauty, especially beauty. When decisions are theirs, directors invite new directors and elect chairmen they think won't confront them. (Sometimes, they get it wrong.) Rarely are people with so little personal respect or affection for each other so delightfully collegiate as they can be on company boards.

My last interview for the job at Cement was with Chris. On the far side of his rounded office window, across the intersection of cars on roads and pedestrians on footpaths, was the Rag & Famish Hotel, North Sydney. I didn't mention it in a job interview.

Chris was deceptively average in height and a little sturdier than most in build. Aged in his low to middling fifties, evenings on his motor boat and weekends piloting gliders kept his face and arms tanned. Most of his South African accent had faded from the voice that penetrated where his studying eyes couldn't reach. He'd been an engineer, who'd become chief executive of a fertiliser company before it merged with another fertiliser company, making him redundant and richer.

I was impressed that a chief executive would interview me sitting on a sofa in his office, dressed as Chris was. His flannelette shirt was much like the shirts I'd worn as a ragged university student. His open collar was nearly enough to make me think I should remove my tie. His trousers were lazy, grey-blue cotton, much like the trousers I wore to mow lawns or pull out weeds from the garden. He didn't need to market himself to me. I was the job applicant marketing myself to him.

Wearing my white cotton shirt as corporate lawyers wore to interviews, my tie with a nondescript pattern offered enough colour to be interesting without garishness, flamboyance, or flippancy. (Not that I recall which tie it was, but every tie I wore to job interviews was like that.) My best dark, double-breasted suit was a gift from my aunt after my suits had become worn. During my twenty months a novelist, they'd also become fodder for silverfish. On my feet were the black leather shoes with brass buckles I'd bought long ago working in London. On Chris' feet were sloppy, brown loafers, resting against the corner of a coffee table.

If Chris or any of the people who'd already interviewed me asked the reason I wanted the job, I'd have talked eagerly about enjoying my work as a lawyer and about the job drawing upon my experience but still giving me something new. The recent merger forming Cement Australia, I told Chris, was a chance to do things as well as they could be done: choosing from the better of each way the two premerger companies operated or something better anew. Something I said, or didn't say, was enough for Chris to approve the company hiring me to be company secretary and, in effect, general counsel.

In deciding whom to recruit, Chris used to choose applicants who worked on their cars, although the jobs had nothing to do with cars. Such a condition might seem to be gender discrimination, but I could never work on a car beyond adding petrol and occasionally oil, water, and air. The people Chris wanted to employ were self-reliant, more practical than artistic or idealistic, and enjoyed manual (and even menial) labour rather than intellectual rigour. It was discrimination by character.

Chris might've been the first chief executive to enunciate so clearly that character was a condition to getting a job, although he mentioned it well after I joined Cement, during an executive meeting. Chris' criterion waned as cars became so technically complex only mechanics understood them. We paid others to perform manual tasks anyway.

Late one year through my time at Cement, a fellow attendee at a Graduate Management Association of Australia Christmas party told me he'd assisted Macquarie Bank in recruiting university graduates. The only absolute prerequisite to applicants obtaining a job there was that they'd worked for at least two years while they studied. The work could have been nailing waste blocks of wood pointlessly together, but a university medallist without it wouldn't be offered a job. Applicants' willingness to work very long hours mattered more than their marks.

Among my wife's colleagues when she worked as a schoolteacher was a head of department who wanted the school to hire an assistant for her. She said the ideal candidate would be "not too clever, someone who'll do what they're told."

Some managers simply don't want to appoint anyone cleverer than they are. That can leave very few.

It will almost always exclude the cleverest. When a German Jewish bank made an accountant Anthony, the most talented of its project financiers and manager of its resource finance team in Sydney, redundant, he expected to find a new job easily, but none of the ten or so people he'd previously trained offered him a job. Only one responded to his application, with the rare honesty to say he couldn't hire Anthony because Anthony could do his job better than he could.

A decade later, on the last Tuesday in May 2008, I met Anthony at the office opening for a small uranium exploration company. A divorcee raising children at school, he worked only four and a half days a week as company secretary and chief financial officer for a few small public companies.

In May 2015, Anthony was again unemployed, having applied for fifty jobs without being awarded so much as an interview. He was also the only person I've heard suggest that parenthood could help a person through my working life get a job. Being fifty-three years old with no mortgage and his children out of school, he was financially independent. Anthony believed employers wanted employees with dependent spouses and children making them financially dependent upon their incomes, because they couldn't afford to stand up to improper conduct by their colleagues and illegal demands by their superiors.

Sometimes, all knowledge does is teach us right from wrong, but employers don't want right from wrong. They want obedience.

The supposed rewards of our long education proved elusive. To succeed in corporate careers earning much money, we need to leave our intellects behind. Profitless philosophers were sent home to think about gardening, while moneymaking automatons rose through company ranks.

When I imagined my non-fiction writing could form a university thesis, I attended an information session back at the Macquarie Graduate School of Management. Also in the audience, a student for a Doctor of Business Administration degree said that such a high level of study was the worst thing he could do for his company career. Employers wouldn't dare hire anyone too clever. Rather than admit to studying those few years and acquiring his doctorate, he said he'd be better telling prospective employers he'd been in gaol.

5

The Corporation as a Cult

Businesspeople used to enjoy grandiose business ventures, much like those that inspired us at TNT, before too many companies like Holyman suffered disasters and there came to be so many accountants. Otter enthused for little more than its mines reaching milestones of production, for which it produced black polo shirts suitably embossed. Tribalism became another management tool.

Having been the company secretary at the northern premerger company that became part of Cement for more than two decades and by then sixty-five years old, Ron could've taken his redundancy package and retired (the inaugural internal auditor was surprised that he didn't), but he needed money to fund his teenage daughter training and riding horses. When I heard, at my first interview at Cement, the acting incumbent was among the five interviewees for the new company secretary role, I assumed I had no chance of success. Ron didn't have a Law degree.

Gary told me later that not appointing his friend with whom he'd worked for seven years was among the most difficult decisions he'd made. Within a few days of me starting work there, on Monday, the fifteenth day of September 2003, the announcement went out to all employees of Ron's departure. So kind were Gary's words about Ron, I felt like I shouldn't be there. "I wanted it to go out before you started," Gary told me, in the office we shared.

To provide Ron the income he needed to support his daughter's horses, Gary had helped create a job for him with the major Swiss shareholder in Brisbane. Gary was never going to last.

The two companies that merged to form Cement Australia were tribes, as old companies often were. New Western companies, like Cement, normally aren't.

Chris stamped out the practice he called "a polo shirt for every occasion," inherited from those old companies. Employees received no perks or other material benefits from the company beyond our fixed annual remuneration. Word quickly spread never to wear the discontinued polo shirts in Chris' presence; I'd accumulated two early in my time there. Keen to avoid contamination, clothes carrying other company names or logos were similarly banned.

Instead, the company issued personal protective equipment, P.P.E., such as bright yellow reflective overalls, required by law to be worn around plants for safety and bearing the Cement Australia logo. Intended to represent two companies coming together and then rising to new heights as one, the logo looked something like a smile. (That was probably an accident. It might've been a smirk.)

Mouse pads were embossed with the logo. So eventually was every company computer screen.

Before Wayne's arrival, human resources personnel bequeathed by the two premerger companies were generally harmless: a few clerks at a handful of sites paying employee salaries and otherwise trying to assist. The sense of belonging in a company is inversely proportional to the number of human resources personnel.

Wayne started work at Cement a little more than two weeks after I did, after I'd accepted the company's invitations to start earlier than we'd hitherto agreed and he didn't. I'm not sure how I knew he was a few years older than I was, for there was no trace of grey in his fair brown-auburn hair. His thick skin slightly tanned, Wayne strode through the offices with a military air reminiscent of the New Zealand Army in which he'd trained. Such intensity seized his face, I thought I should salute. If he really was raised on a South Island farm, it wasn't obvious.

Much of my work was a compromise towards an ideal. Wayne supported my proposal to the executive committee for a legal panel, for which I dutifully empanelled the two lawyers he'd long briefed on employment issues. When he was running late to our first Christmas party, aboard a boat in Sydney Harbour, he telephoned me to say so. Wayne, the second youngest executive to me being the youngest, appeared a like-minded friend.

Yet, Wayne was no less dismissive than Chris of what Chris called nanny states and old-fashioned companies like the two that merged to become Cement, looking after their residents and employees. The northern premerger company provided employees gymnasium memberships. The southern premerger company assisted them with their children's education. Chris and Wayne called such employee benefits paternalistic, as if paternity were an insult.

Weaning employees away, fixed annual remunerations replaced a plethora of employee benefits (including superannuation or anything else required by law), leaving only those remote location benefits needed to keep staff where too few people went and accident insurance confined to employees who'd previously worked in the southern premerger company. (Spreading the risk and reducing administration, leaving the latter in place was cheaper than paying the benefit to each individual. Every time one of those employees departed, the company wound back the policy a bit further.)

All employers promise employees is money. That's all employees expect.

Colin, the integration manager responsible for planning the new Cement head office, initially allocated me only a workstation. Gary kept apart from my lobbying for an office, but it's a rare manager who stands by his or her underlings in a company conflict. (There isn't any point.)

That first December, we moved into our sprawling new offices. At our modern big desks we sat between glass fronting walls, solid pale grey side walls, and windows admitting vistas of wide Sydney Harbour: bright, confident blue waters when the merry sun shone; angry buckets of rain and flash lighting when storms hollered down. The central staff kitchen and eating area was a brash, garish orange, visible through a huge rounded passageway and two smaller, round window spaces from the corridors, like the wide mouths of postmodern shouting.

If not the most beautiful, then the offices were certainly the most expensive I'd enjoyed. Behind me at my desk was a view beyond the harbour to some portions of ocean: deep blue horizons beyond undulating tree-filled suburbs of plush homes and apartments. Aside from the crammed office I'd shared with Gary through my first few months at the company (in which my desk was already configured facing a wall perpendicular to Gary's desk), I always set my desks so they faced the doors of my offices. Doing so seemed more welcoming and friendly, I thought. (They also saved me from people startling me from behind or seeing what I was doing on my computer screen.)

Our offices were long with good width, and in mine were the new bookcases and filing cabinets I'd chosen. Among the files, books, and publications I wanted close to my fingertips would stand a malleable soft shark (a gift from the Gilbert & Tobin law firm) and the little wooden puzzle Gary distributed to participants at what would be the only finance division conference he convened, in Noosa.

On the wall, I would hang the certificates of my admission to the Supreme Court and the Institute of Chartered Secretaries and Administrators, with scrolled lettering more impressive than my university degrees. Like almost everything public in our company careers, they weren't so much matters of pride as matters of marketing: marketing me. I was employed to be expert and they evidenced my expertise. (When we don't know whether people are telling us barmy old drivel, we trust their qualifications.)

In the late 1980s, critics normally unconcerned about rules of language criticised Liberal Party leader John Howard for seeming to create a new word: incentivation. That politically charged criticism didn't prevent Colin, two decades later, speak of "incentivising" people at Cement. (Thankfully, my Microsoft word-processing computer software didn't recognise those words.)

We adopt what we think is any new word to connote sophistication and science, provided the term doesn't sound *too* scientific. There was hardly a more ubiquitous new word than "proactive," and hardly a person who used it more often than Colin. I asked him what the word meant, as against simply being "active." With his voice rising and stressing that first syllable, he insisted it meant being "*pro*active."

Complicated niche words, if they can be called words, had also become commonplace; the more complicated the better. Most industries, professions, and even some companies create their own language: business-speak; industry-speak. The cement industry created the word "cementitious" to describe products customers could readily substitute for cement. It wasn't a word for the rest of the world, not even those customers.

Late in 2003, soon after Cement was formed, the directors defined the company's hallowed Vision 2006, "*To be the leader in Bulk & Packaged Cementitious Products (Cement, Flyash, Slag) in Eastern Australia.*" There were seven specific items refining that vision, a sort of pathway to heaven, including such inspirational goals as a twenty percent return on net operating assets. Chris told employees that the vision wasn't targeted to 2006 because that was when his contract of employment expired. (He was probably joking.)

There hadn't been much diversity at the first three companies at which I worked as a corporate lawyer, except in character and values. Personal opinions were no issue at all. When values came to matter so much that we based our decisions upon them, judging people by their values as we don't judge them by anything physical or intellectual about them, values became ideologies.

Beneath Cement's Vision 2006 was what Chris called the "Values," which the executive drafted during two days at the Retreat Hotel, Wiseman's Ferry in January 2004. God issued Ten Commandments. Cement needed only five:

"*SHE (Safety Health Environment): I take responsibility for our safety, health and environment.*

"*People: I respect myself and others.*

"*Customers: We meet our customers' needs.*

"*Add Value: I add value to the business in everything I do.*

"*Shareholders: Our relationship with our shareholders is sacred.*"

Little discussion preceded the initial two items, while I (being a good executive) argued away from maximising quality to just meeting customers' needs. I particularly promoted the fourth value, having observed employees at previous companies for which I'd worked forever finding new bits of pointless work to perform. Chris particularly promoted the fifth, conscious always of who appointed him and determined his salary, bonuses, and other terms of employment.

The company excluded unbelievers, while embracing the faithful. Potential employees would adopt the company values as a condition of any job offer, but dealing with existing employees required a semblance of consultation. General managers presented the values to the next level of managers, who laid them out to the next, throughout the organisation.

In two rare moments of corporate democracy, if only about language, Chris eventually acquiesced to employee complaints about the word "sacred." The fifth value became, "*I match the commitment our shareholders have made.*" The values came to be renamed "Guiding Principles." Employees insisted values were theirs, but the creed of the company was too.

Anyone reflecting those guiding principles could be a fine person to be sure, but the diversity we promote in our workplaces doesn't reach to values. There's no tolerance of contradictory values, whatever anyone calls them. We committed ourselves to upholding the guiding principles and challenging any employees, including executives, who didn't. Employees unwilling to commit to a guiding principle should leave the company.

We didn't allow employees to determine our values. Our values determined our employees.

Values were a reason to discriminate between applicants for a job or promotion and to dismiss employees. Discrimination by values was lawful, as few bases for discrimination in employment still were. It made the guiding principles like laws.

There was always a story to tell about Cement Australia, although the story took a while to unfold. At first it was about Western corporations becoming like cults, for our executives and employees practically chanting our values. All we lack are sheets to wear and flowers to hold.

The West is fixated with values. We think they make morality and religion superfluous.

The story unfolded several times over. Some stories are like that.

The inaugural Cement leadership conference launched the Vision and Values. With several new recruits aboard, Wayne's growing human resources division was bursting into a gallop. Wayne convened the conference where the seventy or so delegates couldn't slip in or away: on an island.

Attendance for invited delegates was compulsory at each company conference, causing great issue two years later when the Gladstone plant manager's wife was due to give birth at the time of the third leadership conference. What would've been a gross dereliction of commitment to the company (a breach of the fourth and fifth guiding principles) was averted by the baby's good sense to arrive before the conference began.

For three days beginning the day before April Fools' Day 2004 (coincidentally, I'm sure), banners with the Cement name and logo hung over the railings at the Couran Cove Resort, South Stradbroke Island. What boatloads of holidaymakers unconnected with, and until then probably unaware of, Cement Australia, made of them, I don't know.

For us, the conference was grand and impressive, with daily or twice-daily chronicles, guest speakers, stalls, exhibits, and souvenir satchels and bags. (The human resources division got away with all sorts of expenses no other division could make.) Delegates received drink flasks adorned with the Cement logo. I'd never before realised companies could commission bottles of sunscreen cream with corporate logos, although the Cement logo was small and practically subliminal.

Chris' prohibition on company polo shirts didn't prevent us receiving caps emblazoned with "*Vision 2006*." Delegates broke into small groups named "breakout groups," as if anyone could, to develop ideas for implementing the vision. Employees developed five specific actions for implementing each guiding principle. My speech launching a trade practices compliance programme was true to it all: insisting employees never need do anything more than comply with the law, while chasing complete market share.

In case employees merely pretended to believe the new faith, or suffered any doubt, the company reinforced their convictions. The human resources division and executives repeated the Vision 2006 and guiding principles with unending inculcation. Computer screen savers would eventually become slideshows of images and captions of the five guiding principles. Competence and incompetence were less important than was placing a hand on the employee heart and vowing aloud to implement the directors' vision and uphold the five esteemed guiding principles. There was, in short, a persistent underlying hysteria about the company purpose and principle: our reasons for being.

The leisurely setting might've helped me set myself apart from it all and observe, as no other executives or employees apparently did. Around us were tourists swimming and boating, while sitting with me in the sun by the blue holiday waters, on a broad, brown timber deck where people ought to relax, were a trade practices lawyer Ian and the Cement people and brand manageress Monica. (Only human resources divisions come up with titles like people and brand manager.) In my hand was most likely a cold bottle of Corona beer, a thin slice of lime squeezed through the open bottleneck. "Without religion anymore," I said, or words to such an effect, "companies have become like cults."

Older than I was, Ian concurred. One of Wayne's highly skilled new recruits and much younger than I was, Monica didn't. University educated in Law among other disciplines, she often worked late in her office and at home, but she'd not seen what companies and countries once were.

With every sense of ritual from old tribes and religion, representatives of major Cement sites stood before that inaugural leadership conference exchanging gifts with each other: two site representatives before one session, another two before another, and so on. Those gifts were typically long frames of colourful photographs, picturing the donor's office, plant, or depot. The ceremony was their induction into the newly formed company.

The recipients took the gifts they received back to the sites where they worked and displayed them, teaching their colleagues a little about those other sites and binding them together. If ever they visited those other sites and recognised the gifts their workplace representatives had given, they should feel more bonding. They should thus all feel bonding with the whole of the company to which they belonged, until they were fired.

6

The Corporation as Words

Vision means seeing what's already there or what isn't but could be, with the wisdom to know the difference. My eight-year-old eldest son confidently assured me that Cement Australia had a vision, because he'd seen it on a cap I'd brought home from that first leadership conference. I explained to him that only people without vision need to keep insisting they have one.

Cement had operated a public computer website since before I'd heard of the company, where preparing for my first job interview I found small pages of colourless detail about the company and cement, designed as much for schoolchildren completing their homework as anything else. Like so much else it reinvented, the new human resources department replaced the site with bright, colourful new motions and features making everything feel fresh, launched with glossy, small cards distributed to everyone it could.

The new site taunted viewers with the icon *"Employee Login,"* requiring secret user names and passwords. Knowing how easily employees could print documents and anonymously forward them out of the company, I only placed on the company's internal computer network (the intranet) material I wouldn't care if the world could see.

The secrets that matter are personal. Cement calculated annual employee bonuses by formulae reflecting profit, safety results, and, for ten percent of the bonuses, personal achievement. These Short Term Incentive Scheme bonuses were applied as percentages of each employee's annual remuneration, capped at amounts up to thirty percent. Only a careless word from one general manager in an executive committee meeting revealed to me that the bonuses paid to Chris and the general managers were uncapped. (The chief financial officer was considered a general manager.)

I alone among the executives was not a general manager. My bonus was capped.

Brazenly lying, a draft booklet explaining the bonus system said expressly there was no Long Term Incentive Scheme at Cement. I knew from board meetings there was such a scheme, restricted to Chris and the general managers. Only I, to my knowledge, pointed out that saying nothing was better than lying. Before the booklet was printed and distributed, the reference to a Long Term Incentive Scheme disappeared.

Chris continued to be generally cheerful, while maintaining the barriers around him. Executive biographies on the company website detailed our roles at the company, past jobs, education, and sometimes national origins. Like most executives, Chris made no mention of being married (which he was), or having children (which he had, at least one child anyway). They mightn't have been important to him.

Not that privacy means a person is shy. To urinate, Chris didn't stand facing the toilet as other men did. He stood to the side, with the cubicle door wide open. His voice bellowed out in the conversation he made, as he displayed his grasped manhood.

If I ever saw Chris the afternoon of Melbourne Cup Day, the first Tuesday each November, then it was the first Cup Day we each worked at Cement. Melburnians enjoyed a public holiday and across the rest of Australia, people who rarely gambled bought sweepstake tickets. Workers in factories and offices, students at schools and universities (although not those sitting examinations), and patrons in bars and restaurants turned their attention briefly to Flemington Racecourse, casting their eyes towards television sets and ears toward radios. Up to twenty-four thoroughbreds bolted thirty-two hundred metres around a grass track, while people who rarely drank Champagne (or even the sparkling wine we called champagne) did so that day, albeit it from plastic long-fluted glasses at the initial Cement Australia head office. It was my first Cement social event.

Soon afterwards, the newly appointed Wayne and I attended a meeting in Sydney city. Returning to the street to hail a taxi, Wayne mentioned to me, "Bob and I were horrified."

Bob was the general manager for safety, health, environment, and quality. I imagined what evil they'd encountered: theft, fraud, corruption?

Wayne explained, "Serving alcohol in the office!"

Later, in a brief aside near the office building lifts where no one else saw us, I mentioned Wayne's words to Bob. "Wayne keeps saying that," sighed Bob, "but I don't mind alcohol in offices." There was no machinery more dangerous to operate in an office than a coffee percolator or photocopy machine.

Wayne might've feared alcohol diminishing employees' focus on work, releasing emotions they carefully controlled, or worst of all risking honesty and openness. In any event, the issue was less about alcohol than about Wayne. If Wayne thought he needed to claim an ally in Bob, then he wouldn't need that ally for long.

It took several months, well after we'd moved into the new head office, before rampaging Wayne banned alcohol from all company premises. The large Milton office conducted an auction of all alcohol there (without a liquor licence), I later discovered, donating the proceeds to charity.

Wayne spoke of pouring down the sink any alcohol he found at head office. When next I found the boardroom empty, I quietly opened the credenza doors to remove the bottles of wine and spirits I knew were there. Most had already gone, pilfered by one or more of my colleagues thinking as I thought. What remained included a bottle of sparkling wine, with the uninspiring caption "*Champagne Taste on a Beer Budget.*" The business park that donated it had slapped on the label its cryptic logo, "*l+e+q+a=Waterloo Business Park,*" and a picture of a three-storey office building for lease.

Also in that cupboard were several commemorative stone jars of port, produced several years earlier for the southern premerger company. The port tasted worse than I should have expected it to taste. (That was presumably why, when I opened those credenza doors, it was still there.)

Three years later, I risked the sparkling wine. It made me reminisce for the port.

One rumour was that Chris would've liked to enjoy alcoholic drinks on a Friday afternoon in the office, but wasn't willing to confront Wayne on the issue. Sure, Chris wanted to be seen to be friendly and Wayne wanted to be seen as a tyrant, but it seemed to me Chris was too forceful a person for the rumour to be true. His friend Martin, initially working there as a consultant, didn't believe it. After his sudden demotion from being sales and marketing general manager, Shaun said he "knew it was a bad sign when they stopped having drinks."

A year after Wayne's arrival, Cement acknowledged the Melbourne Cup with a sweepstake and orange juice around the boardroom television set. Another year later, in spite of the sweepstake, employees remained at their desks.

People in big companies don't need Melbourne Cup festivities anyway, not with company conferences. No less impressive than the annual Cement senior leadership conferences became the annual divisional conferences, also convened by Wayne's ever-expanding human resources division. Spreading corporate messages further throughout the company, they offered pencils, vinyl folders for notepads, and rulers with the company logo.

From the second annual leadership conference onwards, the company presented Awards for Excellence for each guiding principle to teams across the organisation. An additional Managing Director's Award, made at Chris' discretion, recognised a team of employees demonstrating all five guiding principles. Representatives of each winning team addressed the conference with their personal testaments of what their work and the guiding principles meant to them: journeys towards salvation. The audience of employees (knowing they were being watched as much as were the people at the podium) clapped enthusiastically. At any moment, someone could have started speaking in tongues.

Winning the awards came with no cash prizes or other tangible benefits, which could've become motivations to win instead of a deep, heartfelt yearning to demonstrate the guiding principles. Along with the kudos and accolades was presumably a warm glow in the soul much as the Apostles must've felt spreading similarly good news. A large, clear, rectangular acrylic trophy, emblazoned with the company name and logo and incorporating a caption identifying each award and winning team, remained permanently at the site where the winning team was based, further inspiring employees to keep doing more to live by the company lore.

The company required not just employees to share its guiding principles but also major suppliers, calling them partners when they did. A purchase was normally much briefer than employment (although not much briefer in the case of some employees).

In 2005, the human resources division produced a twelve-page glossy company brochure. Filling the first pages were a photograph and words of introduction from Chris, with a heading emblazoned across them decreeing him as "*Visionary*." Thankfully, the article didn't go on to describe his birth to a virgin mother. Nor did the company go so far as to erect three-metre-high bronze statues of him.

Chris was a sort of high priest, travelling from the towered head office cloister to all major sites every three months in what he called the Quarterly Road Show. Around him at least one executive would always be present, reflecting Chris' desire not to be seen as being single-handedly the executive. (The fact that he was single-handedly the executive made it even more important that he *not* be seen to be single-handedly the executive.) Like all good sermons, the hour-long sessions complete with presentations from overhead projectors offered a theme every time, tied to a guiding principle or two.

Employees not directly and compulsorily engaged in their roles were compelled to attend. Merely being busy with work and already knowing the substance of what Chris would be saying did not excuse the second internal auditor from attending one presentation. More important than the most brilliant of analyses, strategies, and reports, a poor performance review criticised Stuart for not fitting in with the organisational values. His role was reviewing all other parts of that huge organisation. The human resources division's role included reviewing him.

Also quarterly came the magazine that Wayne insisted *not* be a magazine of "births, marriages, and deaths." (He'd never experienced more than one of them himself. He mightn't have experienced any.) Every article among the dozen or more in each edition espoused Cement's achievements, tying them to one or more guiding principles. In spite of a competition among staff to determine a name for the magazine, Chris named it *Vision*, ensuring it would be more of the process driving employees to attaining Vision 2006 and whatever vision succeeded it.

All employees received copies mailed to our home addresses. Like pornographic magazines, we dutifully claimed to read and be inspired by the articles, while studying only the magnificent photographs.

Also receiving them were people associated in any small way with the company, including an insurance broker lobbying for the Cement account I'd befriended at Holyman and Otter and added to the distribution list. As Colin S pointed out, the articles meticulously avoided conveying any substantive information about the company or anything else. (That was no less true of the article I drafted about the trade practices compliance programme I'd implemented.)

As if all that weren't enough, the human resources division endlessly produced and distributed highly choreographed short films (with bouncy music and extensive camera changes) describing the Awards for Excellence winners and other company stories promoting the glorious guiding principles. The Australian cinematic film industry must've been in quite a parlous a condition at the time, with the most talented film-makers taken up with Cement.

By the third year of leadership conferences, peppy music pumped up the delegates as we entered and departed each session. Unfortunately, all copies of a film exhorting the virtues of the packaged products division had to be hurriedly retrieved from the delegates. Somebody had realised the people development manageress (people development being what human resources people called training) was looking at the camera and talking while seeming to drive a car: a clear violation of the guiding principle promoting safety. In fact, she hadn't been driving, but the artistic film-makers made it seem that she was.

The plant employee who'd drawn the human resources department's attention to Jim Collins' book *Good to Great* delivered his testament about how the book inspired him in his work. (Many years later, Stephen became a general manager; he knew the road to success.) Our conference packages included copies of the book in much the same way hotels used to offer guests Gideon Bibles. Unlike the hotels, the human resources division told us to read these books and share them with our team members back at our workplaces. (I don't know if anyone did.)

None of the company films or magazine articles was about individual employees. None of the Awards for Excellence were awarded to individuals. Doing so would create status for individuals rather than the company, vision, and guiding principles.

The pictures around company offices (including, but not only, those exchanged with other sites) were of plants and furnaces, mines and minerals, and occasionally nondescript men in hard hats. Amidst them but dominating the white walls of the head office reception area were words from among the five great commandments set forth in huge lettering: "*Safety, People, Customers, Value, Partnerships.*"

The company creed had broadened with the final guiding principle becoming "*Partnerships: I work closely with others for mutual benefit.*" Two years after the directors enunciated Vision 2006, the directors and executive (of which I was no longer a part) superseded it with simply, the Vision.

Overarching the vision and guiding principles, executives developed the company branding as "*Competitive, Caring, and Collaborative.*" Five fine guiding principles gave way to three fine characteristics. The guiding principles were values, but the branding was character. We'd come to a more complete sense of what Chris required when long ago he wanted employees who worked on their cars.

The 2006 leadership conference instructed every delegate to cease "off-brand behaviour," to conduct a "self-brand audit," and to adopt "brand language." Small groups of delegates discussed examples of the company already demonstrating the branding, before brainstorming means to integrate and communicate the brand in our work environments every day. All delegates made written personal commitments to perform five actions as "brand leaders."

When all marketers did was brand products and services, branding distinguished particular products or services from others. If branding companies is supposed to distinguish them from others, then branding Cement as competitive, caring, and collaborative presumed that other companies weren't, in that industry at any rate. Other companies professed one or two of those traits, but not all of them. In combination those traits were unique to Cement.

They weren't. Other companies claimed the same traits with different words.

Words defined and refined all the companies. They defined the people who worked at them: directors, executives, and employees alike.

Cement's human resources department and its multitude of collaborative consultants nominated each other, but were rightly the recipients of several awards. Their achievement was particularly impressive, because so much of what they said was untrue.

7

The Corporation as a Police State

There was no end of consultants at Cement Australia, many of them procured by the ballooning human resources department. Admittedly Glen Thomas, the supply chain general manager, said of one that he was "not just a consultant. He gives good advice."

For all the hoopla of visions, guiding principles, and branding, Chris and the general managers spoke of individual employees working for particular general managers, as if they were in the general manager's personal employ. In effect, they were. The general managers were accountable for outcomes charged to them by Chris. Every employee within his division was the means by which the general manager succeeded and employee failed. The result was the silos in which Chris complained people worked.

Chris managed every company operation by means of his monthly executive meetings, discussing all manner of detail. An array of presenters passed through, reporting on safety incidents or anything else before being brushed back out again. Chris wanted the minutes to record his decisions as executives' resolutions. I complied. Meetings began (as was customary) with executives adopting my draft meeting minutes as accurate records of past meetings. Their silence was their concurrence.

The corporate politic is somewhere to hide, whenever accountability threatens to harm us. Chris submitted nothing material to the board without executives' prior review, devolving accountability for his decisions from one man to none.

One of the first executive committee meetings I attended expended an hour discussing Chris' plan to block company computers accessing the public computer network (the internet) because employees might use them for personal matters. Each executive in turn around the table, Chris staring him down, had to explain why his work required access. Fortunately, I'd needed that day to check the securities commission or some similar site (as well as reading the news, tending to my banking, or whatever). Gary said to me afterwards, "That was a complete waste of time!"

Sometime during each meeting, Chris trained his eyes around everyone in the room, checking each executive was coming to dinner with him at a local restaurant that night. The only good excuses for not coming were those about work. As Gary once remarked, "My idea of a good time is not being ordered to have dinner with Chris...."

Soon, there came monthly sales and operations committee meetings involving all executives and the supply general manager, although they consumed only the mornings. Between the two meetings each month, nothing much escaped the fortnightly gatherings.

Many a person's mind wanders from the meetings in which he sits, unless matters affect her personally. In the boardroom of the new offices, fortunate participants sat where we could look past the dedicated faces on the far side of the table towards the harbour, ocean, and sky.

As time progressed, the executive committee came to review lists of employees using laptop computers and mobile telephones. Only employees needing them for work retained them.

Every month, the committee reviewed the list of employees (other than general managers) with the ten highest mobile telephone charges the previous month. General managers ensured that employees from their divisions who appeared on the list reduced their mobile telephone usage. Wayne needed only to tell anyone from his human resources division that he didn't want to see that employee's name on the list again.

Purchases of palm-held organisers were suspended for three years, while the company carefully assessed its requirements. Their eventual trial use was confined to executives.

If that close overseeing seemed like a reason for employees to leave, Chris and his lieutenant Wayne forbade employees from discussing future employment with any of the company's three shareholders except with Chris or Wayne's prior permission. Claiming to act in those employees' best interests, employees should then leave everything to the Cement human resources division. Several employees (including me, late in my time there) dutifully entrusted ourselves to it. Aside from Wayne when he eventually wanted to work for the Swiss shareholder, the division never secured anyone a job.

It was much like the old Soviet Union and East European communist countries sealing their citizens behind the Berlin Wall and barbed wire of the Iron Curtain. Chris and Wayne never stopped fuming at the inaugural internal auditor after he secretly secured a job for himself in Switzerland. When a guest dinner speaker from the neutral Swiss shareholder told delegates to my final finance division conference they should liaise directly with anyone they knew in the shareholder if they wanted to work there, Chris rushed Wayne to the conference to tell delegates, as soon as the guest had gone, to ignore what their guest had told them.

Gary had been chief financial officer at the northern premerger company and among only three people entrusted with negotiating the highly secretive merger forming Cement. They'd been difficult months he'd kept hidden from his friends, like Ron, before he went onto become the inaugural chief financial officer at Cement.

He was intelligent and personable, exacting in his standards without abuse or derision. "I hire good people," he told me, "and let them get on with their jobs." (Obviously, I like to think every person who hired me hired good people. They all let me get on with my job, even if others didn't.) The tasks to complete were important, or so they seemed at the time, while we enjoyed undertaking them.

Sharing a crammed office with Gary through my first few months at Cement helped me learn much about the organisation. It also taught me that Gary was taking his granddaughter to see *The Lion King* musical; he was young to be a grandfather. Gary maintained every business confidence while, over dinner before the first finance division conference, he and his wife told me every detail of their courtship. (I had asked, after all.) Working with Gary was so good I imagined being there until I retired, as Ron had tried to do.

Gary did everything too well for me to notice Wayne organising a "three-sixty degree study" of him (the sort of study from all three hundred and sixty degrees around a person the manuscript assessor commenting upon *Western Individualism* must have wanted). External consultants interviewed Chris, Gary's fellow executives, and everyone reporting to him. I had only compliments to make about Gary, as had everyone to whom I spoke about it afterwards. If the study was anything more than another of the grandiose studies and schemes the all-encroaching human resources division undertook, then surely Gary was marked for still higher roles.

When Gary mentioned his wife was away for the week, I invited head office staff to join us for a drink that Friday night (the night before the Queen's Birthday long weekend). Only the business improvement manager did, in the outdoor sitting area of the Greenwood Hotel, below the tall office buildings including the one in which we worked hard every day. A year had passed since the merger forming Cement.

At eight o'clock Tuesday morning, before I arrived in the office after the holiday Monday, Chris and Wayne fired Gary. He left the office without speaking to anyone, although Chris informed each of us that morning that Gary was leaving the company.

The consultants' report apparently justified his dismissal, although I never saw the report and don't know anyone who did. (Chris and Wayne mightn't have bothered, unless to check the consultants understood their brief.) Wayne forthrightly told me, "I will never be caught out on due process," by which he meant the laws and practices governing employee dismissals. (Cement was, initially, more concerned with procedures than was any other company for which I'd worked.)

Gary's dismissal unleashed a flood of insecurity through me. If there'd been an inkling it was coming, then I could've relied upon there being no sign of me being dismissed to feel no concern. If someone as skilled and dedicated as Gary could be summarily fired, so could anyone.

I telephoned Gary at home. "How are you feeling?" I asked him.

He said he was fine. I didn't believe him.

Gary said Chris wanted a chief financial officer more broadly an executive than Gary wanted to be. The announcement to staff said Gary wanted to return home to Queensland.

That evening, Wayne invited several people to revel with him at the familiar (at least to me) Rag & Famish Hotel, where he told an employment lawyer (and golf photographer), that he and Chris that day had dismissed so senior an executive as a chief financial officer. Mimicking American sportsmen and their "high five," Wayne and the lawyer exuberantly raised their arms and slapped the palms of each other's hands. When Wayne added that the man dismissed without warning had come into the office to work that past long weekend, the lawyer and he laughed.

Ironically, Gary had often complained his head office colleagues had "no idea how to have fun." Wayne did that night at the Rag.

Gary didn't know Wayne had so celebrated when, a week later, he and his wife ate a farewell dinner with Wayne, his and Chris' secretary Sueki, and me at a waterside restaurant. At the end of the night, leaving the taxi outside the offices we'd shared, I shook Gary's hand. "Thank you for a great nine months," I said sadly to him. It all seemed very short.

A rumour credited the Australian American shareholder customer with wanting Gary dismissed, because he'd argued with that shareholder's chief financial officer. (Amidst secrecy, rumours abound.) The explanation was believable, until half a year later. Wayne told me Chris dismissed Gary because, whenever Gary spoke to Chris, Gary lent back in his chair and placed his hands behind his head.

Never mind my work, I was immediately conscious of my stance as I sat and what I did with my arms, checking my hands and elbows. Gary lent back in his chair and placed his hands behind his head whenever he spoke to anyone. For Chris, with his ego more massive and fragile, the posture was unacceptable defiance.

Natural selection might've involved Chris challenging Gary to a fight to determine who should lead the pack, which might've caused Chris to reveal what bothered him about Gary. For Glen Thomas (to whom I mentioned Wayne's words) and me, we knew only to sit low in our chairs with our arms to our sides or in front of us, keeping watch for another three-sixty degree study.

A year later, the employment lawyer who'd laughed at Gary's dismissal and his colleague David (with whom, thirty-two years earlier, I'd played in a schoolboy soccer team for players under eleven years old) shared morning tea with me in the basement café of the Westin Sydney Hotel. With no hands raised in the air or palms slapping, they complained to me of the treatment meted out to them by partners controlling the firm at which they were partners. They soon moved to another firm.

There was a lot to distinguish Gary from Greg. Never was there a man less likely than Greg to place his hands behind his head in a conversation with Chris. Without ambition beyond working as hard and well as he could, I never heard Greg say a bad word about anyone or complain about anything. Without conniving on Greg's part, or even knowledge that Gary was being dismissed, Chris appointed Greg the new chief financial officer.

The business development manager at one Cement joint venture described Chris as "the smiling assassin."

Certainly, Chris smiled when he quoted a director nominated by the Swiss shareholder telling him that, among the Swiss shareholder's directors and employees, Chris was known as a "hard man." Cement executives laughed.

I think it was Wayne who so earnestly referred a Cement executive committee meeting to a Clyde depot employee's use of the racist epithet "nigger." Whether it referred to a particular employee, visitor, or anyone else the subject of a workplace conversation wouldn't have mattered.

Most of the ten or so executives shook their heads. Chris called the word "unacceptable." A model of indiscrimination in everything but character, values, and whatever else suited his individual interest, Chris treated most people equally badly.

Having been the chief executive's personal assistant at the southern premerger company, Sueki was the longest standing employee at head office. Divorced and childless, her little office station was probably all she would ever achieve, although the youngest sister of several older brothers might have never aspired to achieve anything anyway. She was something like fifty years old, with black hair aching to grey and yellow complexion affected by the soft suns of holidays rather than the harsher sun of working or simply walking outdoors.

For good and for bad, chief executives ordinarily abandon office culture to their personal assistants. Norm, the southern premerger company chief executive, was no ordinary chief executive. After five employees left the tiny head office because Sueki bullied or dismissed them, Norm told her, "The next person who leaves because of you, you will follow." (The time would come I'd have liked to feel free to tell Sueki the same thing.)

The next secretary hired was Dragana, a strikingly tall, young woman whose height accentuated the girlishness in her manner. With a degree in marketing she'd never used, Dragana was still there when Cement Australia formed, that office became the new company's head office, Norm departed, and Chris became chief executive. Dragana became my first secretary there, reporting also to two other executives.

Sueki called Chris "Boss," with a voice and inflexion like something between a mischievous teenage daughter and a Third World sex worker. She acceded to whatever work he wanted of her, albeit by delegating almost all of it (bar keeping his diary) to other secretaries. I'd have respected Chris and Sueki's characters (although not their tastes) more if I thought they were carrying on a clandestine affair, but I don't think they were. She didn't need them to.

At the same time as he organised the three-sixty degree study of Gary, Wayne orchestrated an external consultant's report into head office operation. In my naïvety, I spoke of all manner of issues, including the benefits of staff sharing drinks together each Friday after work. When asked briefly, almost as an aside, about Dragana, I complimented her ability and attitude. Tucked away part way through

the consultant's long report was the statement recommending
Dragana's dismissal.

The next executive committee meeting discussed no other aspect
of the report. I opposed her dismissal, as later did Greg and Shaun
who'd worked with her at the southern premerger company (after they
again saw her working late in the night). As my experiences of Sueki
unfolded and shortly before his departure, Shaun told me her history.
Almost fondly for times long past, he once referred to her as the Sook.
The name said more about Shaun than it said about her.

Only two aspects of that report into head office operation were
ever implemented. Dragana was promptly dismissed. Henceforth all
secretaries reported to Sueki as head office manageress instead of
executives. The three nice people I'd met the day of my first Cement
interview (Dragana, Gary, and Paul) had all left, essentially
involuntarily, within a year.

My time working with Gary and Dragana had sadly been curtailed.
My time working with Sueki sadly had not.

Sueki bullied her charges. My third secretary, Joanna, told me she
also occasionally invited the young secretaries to lunch, where there
was less an exchange of conversation than Sueki telling them of her
expensive waterfront home and private boat (owned, as it turned out,
by her aged, dying boyfriend) and that she was contemplating early
retirement, not needing to work. Those young secretaries being not as
wealthy as she was, Sueki insisted upon paying for their meals. (People
who aren't rich try hardest to appear rich.) Only Sueki knew if the
company reimbursed her. Getting to a third secretary at Cement didn't
take long.

8

Corporate Totalitarianism

Thomas Keneally's 1982 novel *Schindler's Ark* (known also as *Schindler's List*) described the true story of German Nazi Oskar Schindler, who saved more than a thousand Jews from concentration camps in Poland and Germany during World War II. He maintained a list of supposedly skilled workers, so that Jews who would have otherwise died lived better than did many starving Germans.

Sixty years later, long after the Nazis had been defeated, Wayne maintained what he called "the list," but his list operated the other way around. They really were skilled employees, but Wayne wanted them dismissed. What happened to them after that, he didn't care. At Cement Australia, they numbered as many as thirty-five in a workforce of twelve hundred.

The diversity the company lauded rarely extended to matters of opinion. It never extended to matters of opinion about Chris, Wayne, or where they were taking the company. "He's just not with us," said Wayne amidst a meeting as we sat in his office, marking one complainant for exit without mentioning his name. The complainant had said something critical, late one night in a Couran Cove Resort bar during the first leadership conference.

The shipping manager guessed the person was the Brisbane terminal and grinding mill manager. He was banished to managing an antiquated plant in Rockhampton, the continued existence of which was under review.

There was thus no surprise at the efforts expended by Wayne's human resources division to identify and remove the anonymous scribe who'd written on a wall of the depot in Clyde: "*Chris...is a South African c**t.*" Dismissals weren't limited to people on the list.

Wayne spoke openly of the list, wanting everyone to know it existed. The names on it needed to be kept secret, if every employee was to worry. (Employees suffer more stress from the risk of losing their jobs than watching other employees lose theirs.) When Joanna

51

noticed Wayne's secretary typing it, she was happy enough that her and my names weren't on it.

Craig, the human resources officer responsible for the packaged products and supply chain divisions, was charged with executing most dismissals (other than those of executives), presumably because of his massive and menacing body. The hired assassin, Craig hurried to aeroplanes to fly long distances and dismiss the employees Wayne ordered. The final presentation at one leadership conference offered delegates the chance to grade their experiences of the conference, with the most negative option being that a delegate would prefer an unannounced visit from Craig to attending another leadership conference.

Privately, Craig was friendly and jovial. We talked of his wife, two children, and home on what was essentially a farm beyond the outskirts of Melbourne.

Craig never breached a confidence of which I'm aware, but someone who wondered whether he really enjoyed those tasks he was given was with him in his office the day Wayne telephoned him demanding that he dismiss an employee before five o'clock that afternoon. (Wayne had a loud voice.) Craig replied, "We have to carry out due process."

"I don't care about due process!" roared Wayne. A dutiful underling following orders, Craig dismissed her that afternoon.

Wayne was rarely happier than he was when he learned that companies could dismiss employees upon giving them due notice, excitedly bouncing around the next executive meeting. He wasn't always so measured.

To my knowledge, the only employee on Wayne's list for reasons of incompetence was the affable but clumsy New South Wales transport manager, Neil. (Few employees were dismissed for incompetence in any of the corporations for which I worked.) Being a fellow South African seemed not to have mattered to Chris. It might've mattered to Martin.

Martin was a short man, about sixty years old, with stark, white hair thick on his scalp. He often flew back to South Africa, where much of his wealth remained trapped; every trip was a holiday funded by the little more money he could take away with him each time he departed. A corporate takeover had made Martin redundant, but his wife was a friend of Chris' wife. Together, the four owned a motor boat, which kept Martin's skin a little bit tanned. Soon after Chris was appointed Cement chief executive, he appointed Martin a consultant to the company.

In the crammed conditions immediately after the merger, Martin occupied a desk in Greg's office. The room was configured so that Martin sat facing away from Greg and the door to a window, through which he could gaze across the office-occupied street past dry winter trees to a glass-fronted bank.

When I joined Cement a short time after he did, Martin's was due to leave the following month. Chris extended his consultancy, and the casual conversations we shared when Greg wasn't with him in their office continued. Chris never admitted their friendship, not even when he surprised an executive committee meeting by saying he wanted Martin to join the dozen or so employees briefing executives on the first day of the conference crafting the new company's values. Chris claimed he'd sat by chance beside Martin on an aeroplane (to or from their native South Africa) and been impressed by the man's insight.

Martin's life was much more than working, with his photographs of the holiday home he'd left behind in South Africa. Another photograph pictured him somewhere in snow country, I think, with his friends from the Castrol oil company in which he'd worked long and happily. Proudly, he showed me a copy of a book about Castrol, mentioning him. I'm not sure he spoke to other Cement employees as much as he spoke about them to me.

Rumour was that Wayne's list came to call Martin a *"good guy,"* although it hadn't when first he compiled it. (It wasn't meant to be a list of the good guys.) Wayne would've said as much for no greater reason than learning about Martin's friendship with Chris.

Martin spoke passionately of whatever project he undertook, as the matters on which he advised the company grew. When Greg became chief financial officer, Martin replaced him as the diversified businesses general manager. Within a year, the consultant had become an executive. (Appointing friends is the easiest way for chief executives to command authority over managers.)

So rapid and great was Martin's rise, the environmental manager was overheard complaining that "the only way to get ahead at Cement…was to be a South African owning a boat with Chris…" Stuart R was soon seconded to the cement industry association in Canberra unaware that, Wayne assured me, he would never return to Cement.

Neil, that affable but clumsy transport manager, turned out to have known Martin since long before either joined Cement. Soon, Chris was calling Neil merely "a square peg in a round hole." Appointing Neil a commercial manager in Sydney faced the small complication that the company already had a commercial manager in Sydney. The human resources department carefully planned the sequence of firing the incumbent commercial manager, appointing Neil to the role, and then hiring Neil's replacement.

Still, friendship meant something less than it once had. Martin said Chris "doesn't ever confide in" him about matters of work beyond Martin's role. He believed his friendship with Chris was no more than an opportunity for him to demonstrate his ability. Certainly, Martin was among the most effective (and, not coincidentally, most amicable) businessmen I'd encountered.

Chris sometimes thanked me for work matters as intimate as a memorandum to executives about changes to laws affecting construction sites, but after asking me to arrange a job at a law firm for his daughter, he could never bring himself to thank me. (She thanked me, by electronic mail.) Later, I asked him whether she was enjoying the job, for no other reason than to lead him to speak of it. His reply was to ask me if I'd pulled many strings to procure it. "It helped that" the firm "was on our panel," I told him, "but that'll only get her in the door. She'll do well because of her own ability." Chris said nothing more.

By Martin's reasoning, I'd not done Chris a favour by procuring his daughter a job. I'd merely created an opportunity for her: opportunity without favour. The law firm understood the best way to maximise its work and revenue from Cement and to minimise irritating questions about billing wasn't the quality of its advice, promptness of its provision, or even invitations to lunches, dinners, and art galleries. It was employing the chief executive's daughter.

Away from those things important to Chris, the company was Wayne's World. My secretary Joanna and a mature secretary Gill both believed Wayne's aggression was an act, protecting a frightened, little boy. If they were right, then middle-aged Wayne must've been *very* frightened. In spite of his considerable physical height, he must've felt *very* little.

Among the human resources division employees eating dinner together one evening was Rose. Her lively, animated nature and smile that consumed her thin face were good reason for Wayne to tell her, "You're nice." What left her momentarily speechless was her then telling her. "You're not as nice as Simon Lennon."

Rose, not Wayne, told me what he'd said. That last day of May the year after Wayne and I joined the company, I too was momentarily speechless.

Alone among executives on the company website, Wayne's photograph eventually became a studio-swept pose. Even among so many avowedly private people, none were more private than Wayne. So much as asking a man what he'd done on the weekend, Wayne called an "intrusion upon personal space."

In the closed space of his office, Wayne enjoyed the authority that came with imparting other people's personal information. Long after an executive or other employee had left the company, Wayne divulged all manner of detail about the departure he'd previously concealed. His audience should feel privileged to hear it, although it might've been untrue. (A man isn't less private for what he says about others.)

In a rare moment of personal discourse, one New Year's Eve, Wayne told Joanna he would be watching the Sydney fireworks that night not from the head office windows but from the roof of the building in which he lived. She commented on what must be a good view from harbourside Balmain, to which he quickly responded there could be no more than two people on the roof from each apartment.

Private people prefer the company of strangers who can't recall them when they've left. "I wasn't going to invite myself!" Joanna told me.

Wayne barred all use of badges or labels identifying people's names at Cement, claiming the ban compelled people to speak to each other and remember each other's names. In practice, it meant people forgot them. (That can be useful.) Conversation that might've been more meaningful was deferred by fresh introductions, while people's limited capacity to remember much about others was wasted upon remembering their names.

At a conference convened by the company's Swiss shareholder, Wayne refused to wear the badge allocated to him. He walked away, while a hostess called to him to take it.

Wayne's age was the subject of much speculation, although we supposed he was at least fifty years old. He was unmarried, and came alone to the office Christmas parties. In response to my children, he remarked in another rare instant of levity, walking to our cars in the car park, that he had probably "missed out" on being a father. I wondered what to make of his occasionally clear-varnished fingernails.

As we strolled together around Gladstone early one evening, the people policies and entitlement manager told me Wayne once invited his human resources team to his home. Wayne lived alone.

Few people had photographs at their desks. Martin, Glen Thomas, and the business improvement manager had those of their families. I sometimes did, before a photograph of one or more of my children became my computer wallpaper. At Joanna's desk was a small photograph of her dog Bear, so named for what the great, hairy beast resembled.

Those images were discreet in a professional workplace, but not the photographs in Wayne's office. The shelf below his office window boasted a long gallery picturing him in his travels, with his parents, and with one or more of his siblings. The most intriguing image was of a beautiful woman with long, brunette hair and an engaging smile. Wayne said she was a former girlfriend, who subsequently married somebody else.

Such a photograph in an office was surprising enough. My photographs of former girlfriends, treasured as they are, lie in dark drawers at home. Were I not married they would still lie there, although I might look at them more often than I do.

Wayne's photographs might've been marketing. He might've wanted to seem to be, in some small way, a normal male. In spite of office etiquette preventing observations about anything but work performance and values, Wayne sometimes quipped how beautiful particular women were. Only I heard those quips, wholly unrelated to the conversation beforehand or afterward. His story of a past relationship might've been true, but it revealed nothing about his present personal life. Of that, I might've been better not knowing.

Consultants to the human resources division carried out exit interviews as employees departed; there were several exits. Only voluntarily departing employees were interviewed. Who knew what negative comments involuntarily departing employees might make?

Several voluntarily departing employees spoke of the company maltreating employees, particularly longstanding employees, or otherwise being an undesirable place to work. Wayne and other executives promptly responded by deciding the company was better off without them.

Job applicants normally need references from past employers. We might want to return to past employments someday. Thus, the inaugural internal auditor and a Brisbane-based commercial manager vowed not to sit any exit interview from Cement. All exit interviews could do were soil their relationships with executives, although the auditor's departure to the Swiss shareholder without Chris or Wayne's approval soiled those relationships anyway. The company didn't invite him to sit an exit interview.

Uncompromised by honesty, the most astute departing employees sit exit interviews. They say how wonderful everything is and how much they wish they could stay, and then leave.

Employees see the way the wind blows, learning to recite guiding principles and branding ruthlessly enforced against them. They say what powerful people demand they say, whatever they believe. They stand before audiences keenly lauding what they know they should laud, like participants in an old-God religious revival.

Perhaps, saying what a person doesn't believe lulls him into believing. Affirmations might lull her into not believing anything. It's easier not to think.

In our conversations at Cement, employees were sometimes surprised to admit the company (that is to say, the human resources division) conferences, magazines, computer sites, and presentations were good and useful. (Wayne was very good at his job. He hired very good people.) I'm no longer compelled to say so.

Employees experiencing the Kepner Tregoe process of problem solving and decision making endorsed it, because the human resources division supported it. Perhaps the process was worthwhile, perhaps not. People who've stopped believing their own words are no longer certain other people believe theirs.

Only with longstanding friends or others we knew well did the employees I called dissidents speak freely; I was surprised to learn some of the people not believing what they said publicly. They weren't speaking rudely or crudely, but were unwilling to be seen as not team players: the customary euphemism for describing anybody not wholly convinced of Chris or Wayne's brilliance and integrity. For them, was the list.

9

Corporate Dictatorship

Companies complain that government regulation strangles their businesses. Their human resources divisions strangle their employees. The Cement Australia human resources division developed scores of detailed and colourfully presented policies dictating employee behaviour, displayed upright in racks like magazines to choose. Big companies can be no less bureaucratic than government.

"*Gifts of either goods or services of any nature, regardless of size or value, should be neither accepted nor offered, as a general rule,*" commanded the sixteenth page of the comprehensive Cement code of conduct. "*Where refusal of a nominal gift would be embarrassing or would not enhance the Company's business purposes, acceptance must be made with caution. Full details of the gift should be disclosed to the employee's supervisor or manager.*"

On most head office desks that Christmas were bottles of Champagne from various commercial donors. Receiving mine, I raised the code of conduct with Wayne. (More than actually complying with the code, I wanted to be *seen* to comply.) On Wayne's desk was also a bottle of Champagne. He smiled, and explained that the code didn't take effect until January.

My mother sometimes commanded her children, "Do as I say, not as I do." Nor need company managers comply with the dictates they make.

Among the myriad of edicts distributed by electronic mail, "*Christmas issues*" required sites to spend no more than seventy dollars per employee on Christmas parties, or no more than thirty-five dollars per person if employees could bring guests. Kathryn, a young Brisbane accounts clerk, was thus surprised to see the invoice for the head office Christmas Party (a harbour cruise) come in at something like four times that amount. Kaye, the experienced group accountant, advised her to pay it.

Managers normally keep their non-compliance discreet. To minimise costs, an executive committee meeting resolved that employees fly according to the cheapest fare on a day. Soon afterwards, I had a quiet word with Glen Thomas, whose responsibilities by that time included procurement. As he'd already planned to do for his travel, he exempted mine from the instruction to the company travel agent. Whenever possible, we flew aboard Qantas. Other executives did the same.

There's nothing necessarily wrong with dictatorship; it often works well in military units and film crews. Things come down to what the dictators do: their visions and values.

Among Chris' most perplexing dismissals was that of the inaugural sales and marketing general manager. For seven or so years, the popular Shaun had carried out the role at the southern premerger company, working six days a week. Along with Greg, he'd been one of the few people that company entrusted with negotiating the confidential merger forming Cement.

Shaun's round face grinned as he made cheeky jokes. He also concentrated intensely through thoughtful arguments concerning matters of business, behaving much the same in executive committee meetings as he did sharing the private counsel of his experience. I'd assumed he would in time succeed Chris as chief executive, until the fateful executive committee meeting a year to the day after I started work at the company. Chris announced that Col, whom we'd never met, would become sales and marketing general manager the following Monday.

(Two general managers named Colin might be confusing to read, but it was also confusing at Cement. I call Chris' friend Col in my writing, because Chris addressed him as Col. No one else did.)

While Chris spoke of Col's pending arrival, Shaun sat stony-faced, confessing no feelings at all. He would become responsible for improving and selling a quirky, little plastic-pipe business and reviewing the company operations in Brisbane: trivial tasks as close to being dismissed as Shaun could be, without actually being dismissed. From having more than a hundred people reporting directly or indirectly to him, Shaun would have none.

We met Col for the first time at the executive dinner that evening. Like the ghost who walks, Col's wan skin was the whitest I'd seen since the boy at school known as "Spook." Col's white hair, such as remained, was barely discernible. Conversation with him was strained, with the questions all mine and his answers all brief. I worked hard to extract the information that would ultimately appear at the end of his company website biography: *"Colin is married and has one teenage daughter."*

(Col never again spoke of life beyond work. When he and his wife were pictured in a local newspaper trying to sell his home, I saw she was East Asian. She helped him stand out in the photograph.)

Through the ensuing weeks, Shaun introduced Col to the customers he'd been serving so long, who asked Col why he was there. With Shaun close beside him, Col said he'd wanted to move from cold Britain to warm Australian climes and telephoned his friend Chris asking for a job. Shaun felt a little worse each time he heard Col's reply.

Col said little to his colleagues, so far as I ever heard, but much to himself at his desk. Together, he and Chris related the issues confronting Cement executive committee meetings to their experiences at an industrial gases company where they first worked together.

Keeping his feelings secret from other colleagues, Shaun continued to work hard. Four months into the role relegated to him and the day after the Australia Day holiday, he told me he was "going nowhere, doing dead-end work." Chris tried to create a role for him in Brisbane, but the board didn't support him. Keeping Chris' ego out of negotiations for his way out of the company, Shaun said he treated his situation as a problem for him and Chris to resolve. The company agreed to make him redundant, paying him six months' salary. "It does leave a bad taste in my mouth, I must admit," Shaun told me, the penultimate Thursday in March.

Publicly, Shaun's continued dedication and good spirits led to Wayne describing him as "professional." Professionalism had come to mean working without complaint, no matter how badly a person is treated.

Chris also admired Shaun's professionalism in a speech finally bidding him farewell from the company, the Friday exactly seven months after his demotion. Head office staff gathered in the kitchen and eating area, where Chris presented Shaun with a very large golf club: a driver, with a particularly thick head.

Shaun was much too professional to hit anyone with it, although he did swing it uncertainly through the air. Chris didn't need to hit Shaun anymore.

Unlike any other dismissal, Chris spoke the following year of the company paying Shaun a proportional bonus in excess of that to which company policy and Shaun's deed of release entitled him. Shaun had become general manager of (ironically) a major recycling company. In that role or another, Shaun could one day help Chris or harm him.

Self-interest can make people generous, with other people's money. Wayne supported Cement paying generous termination packages to departing executives, because he saw them trickling along and increasing what he would receive when his time to leave came. He approved the company selling Gary and Shaun's company cars to them cheaply, and reimbursing Gary extra expenses associated with his move back to Queensland. Self-serving morality is morality nevertheless; among the collateral damage our individualism wreaks is some collateral good.

A rumour around Cement was that the company's English shareholder customer had instructed Chris to remove Shaun from his sales and marketing role in retribution for Shaun performing it too well, at the shareholder customer's expense, rather than always indulging it. Most tellingly, the southern premerger company chief executive Norm had defied that same, earlier demand from that shareholder.

Apparently for Norm's loyalty to Shaun and consequent disobedience to that shareholder, the shareholders passed over Norm when choosing a chief executive for the newly merged company. According to the packaged products general manager Peter M and his wife during dinner they hosted me in their home, Norm cried for his loss. Norm retired from work altogether, although he continued sending humorous mail messages to Greg and Shaun. (They kept those jokes to themselves.)

I never met Norm nor spoke with him, but the general managers who'd worked with him spoke well of him. (Sueki never mentioned him.) He demanded much of his executives, but gave much in return. Boarding aircraft early of a morning entitled them to fly business class, so they would arrive at their destinations more relaxed. Norm never expected anyone to do anything he didn't do, while the few head office staff shared a bottle of red wine each Friday night.

Success demands we do what the powerful demand we do. Chris always acquiesced to the three shareholders.

Compliance cascades. Executives acquiesced to Chris. Wayne (described by Shaun as a frustrated chief executive) knew not to debate anything important to Chris.

Provided chief executives are suitably subservient to their boards, according them whatever they desire, chief executives can do pretty much as they like. Provided managers are suitably subservient to their masters and mistresses, according them whatever they want, they can do pretty much as they like.

At the top is absolution. Chairmen of company boards are no more required to follow rules that executives lay down for employees than kings of old were required to follow rules that lords set down for their serfs. They don't need to contribute anything to enjoy absolution. Most of them don't.

Before becoming chairman of the board at Cement, Jerry (not quite his real name, but the chummy name he liked to be called) was managing director of the northern premerger company. Unusually tall and athletically built, he drank exorbitant wine during business trips. To Gary's great surprise, during their time at the northern premerger company, he also expended his own money buying the same wine to take home. "That's really how these people live," Gary told me, among our many conversations through the months we shared an office.

At a little more than fifty years old, Jerry was unusually young to become chairman of Cement. His dinner-time address to the inaugural leadership conference was all about his supposedly grand contribution to the merger forming Cement, as if it couldn't have happened without him. In fact, his managing directorial contribution was simply agreeing to whatever he needed to agree. Gary and other people worked on it.

Professional photographers were constant features of Cement life, organised by the people and brand manageress Monica. For something young Monica once wanted, Sueki called her "precious." (That was when Sueki complained to me about others.)

During one directors' meeting, a photographer set up a small studio in a meeting room near the boardroom. At a break in the meeting, Monica entered the boardroom. With her luscious blonde hair and gently smooth smile, she politely asked Jerry, as chairman, for the directors to come individually into the studio to be photographed. "So, Monica," he sniggered, clearly in breach of the company's guiding principle requiring people to respect each other, "you're going to *do* us one at a time."

Any minor employee would've been sorely reprimanded if not summarily dismissed for such a lewd remark, laced with innuendo. Guiding principles and branding were batons of righteousness to wield, but not upon people more senior.

Monica concealed her fury from him. The photographs for the company website proceeded, but she complained about Jerry's behaviour to Col to whom she reported, Wayne who'd recruited her, and Chris. They all refused to raise her complaint with Jerry. In spite of their pleas for her to remain with the company, Monica resigned.

I learnt of the reasons for her resignation not in any executive committee or board meeting or even head office, but from Peter M based with Monica in Melbourne. Having worked with Jerry at the northern premerger company (including his work with Gary on the merger forming Cement), the supply chain development manager believed Jerry would've been horrified to know he'd upset Monica. No one was willing to ask him.

Enforcing rules against some people but not others is no more unethical than police charging some criminals with crimes but not others. Employees and executives wanting to retain their jobs (let alone be promoted) don't challenge people senior to them.

The values important to unnatural selection aren't those espoused in carefully worded declarations, but those that people observe. Lying removes honesty from the values in play, from the values that might endure.

Executives and employees effectively put aside from our minds the Cement guiding principles in favour of reality principles. Never stated aloud, those words in our heads began something like, "*Acceptance: I will meekly accept without feeling anything I am told to say or do.*" If the human resources division had affixed "*Acceptance*" among the words on the wall behind the head office reception desk, Wayne would've said it meant something else.

If the five Cement guiding principles and three traits of branding didn't make anyone a better person then that didn't matter, for they weren't meant to make anyone better. They were meant to convince everyone we already were what the company brochures said we were. They were company officers and employees marketing the company and our supposed values and characters to suppliers, customers, and communities. They were executives, managers, and employees marketing ourselves to each other. Most of all, we marketed ourselves to ourselves.

In spite of the fanfare, music, and imagery, Cement only ever had three real guiding principles. Nobody expressed them in any vision or values or otherwise listed them together. No one published them on company computer sites, printed them on computer mouse pads, or affixed them to office walls. They weren't part of the company branding, but branding isn't meant to be real. From people with whom I've spoken, they're the same real guiding principles of any company declaring the values and character it claims to possess, and expect of executives, employees, and others.

They were the same corporate dictates that directors at companies for which I'd previously worked came to impose, although those companies never enunciated their visions and values as clearly as did Cement. Even those companies with human resources managers didn't have human resources divisions, let alone one so well resourced and sophisticated as the one at Cement.

When employers recruit team players, they want people who do what they're told. "As you wish," was my phrase for accepting instructions from the Holyman directors, until Griff rebuked me for saying it. He said it sounded like I was merely doing what I was told to do.

Managers insist they don't want "yes people," who simply agree with everything they say. It's true, they don't. They want people who agree sincerely with everything they say, with all our heart, mind, and soul.

Our real guiding principles are the three C's, but not "*Competitive, Caring, and Collaborative.*" They begin with comply and conform. Compliance is a person doing what he or she is told to do. Conformity is doing it without needing to be told. Conformity becomes feeling and thinking what more powerful people expect a person to feel and think, or seeming to anyway.

Those two were the same guiding principles in the long-defunct Soviet Union and under other totalitarian regimes. They're the same guiding principles in a suburban schoolyard and across much of the world, although they're most ironic in our Western multicultural, postmodern democracies. Spruiking diversity in everything else demands conformity in character and values: sameness in diversity.

10

The Corporation as an Asylum

As determinedly as she wanted Dragana removed, Sueki wanted an old filing cabinet to remain. The cumbersome four-drawer safe had been in the southern premerger company offices, although the era in which businesses needed such security for documents had passed. I simplified the document storage system and asked Colin to discard the dark grey monolith when the company moved into new premises. For whatever reason (possibly his knowledge of Sueki), he didn't. The cabinet arrived in Glen Thomas's office, before Sueki dumped it in the only office adjoining a pillar, where the concrete floor was strong enough to support its great weight: mine.

A locksmith opened one of the locks, which could never again be sealed. The ugly, pointless cabinet stood empty. I asked Sueki to remove it, but she insisted it stay. I instructed Dragana and later my third secretary, Joanna, to get rid of it. (My second secretary wasn't there long enough for the instruction.) Sueki ordered each of them to ignore me.

The safe remained. Presumably making some point by doing so, Sueki stored in it a data projector that could've been kept in a cupboard and computer discs already copied to secure sites away from the offices. I tried to perceive the safe as a relic from her past, comforting her in the face of change around her. That perception became harder to sustain.

Bruce had been a colleague of Greg at the company that still officially employed Greg, until that company made Bruce redundant. He then occupied a small desk at the southern premerger company and Cement, quietly fulfilling whatever tasks people gave him. I never heard Bruce speak ill of anyone else, but he said Sueki wasn't very good at her job.

Sueki had always done everything what Greg called "the Sueki way of doing things." Without real work to do, she pored through computer documents I'd created with modern date format and renamed them with archaic formats with which she was accustomed.

Naming computer files by their year, month, and day makes them appear chronologically on computer screens. Naming them by days, months, and years means they don't. Those dates that worked well on paper and blackboards made files and folders much harder to find on computer screens.

I'd explained to Sueki the benefits to her by leaving my formatting in place. That might have made everything worse.

Being head office manageress for the billion-dollar company, Sueki decided that too many employees drank cans of soft drink from the kitchen. "It was meant for guests, but now everybody's drinking it," she complained to me, the second Tuesday in July, less than a year after I'd joined the company. So, she cancelled them.

Wayne prepared to complain that she'd cancelled them when I warned him, "It's been a pleasure working with you."

Having made his mark across the rest of the organisation, Wayne refused to believe he couldn't override a secretary, but the soft drinks never returned. Never again did Wayne disagree with her. Smart people don't wage battles they'll lose.

Two months after the soft drinks ceased, the office receptionist Gisella told me Sueki hid the kitchen biscuits. Fearing that employees were taking fifty-cent postage stamps from Gisella's desk, Sueki instructed her to hide the stamps in a drawer of her desk, inside boxes for sachets of soup.

There was no limit to the grand trivialities: the importance of unimportant things. A year after we'd moved into the new offices, the first Thursday afternoon that following December, Sueki noticed me carrying a round table towards my office. "What are you doing with that?" she complained.

"Colin's looking for a place for it," I sighed, wanting to return to my work at my desk. Col's secretary Jill had already distracted me wanting my help; my errand was a favour to her. "I'm just looking after it until we find another place for it."

Sueki left, but quickly returned. "Colin's table is still there," she told me.

"No, it isn't."

I accompanied her along the corridors to the far corner of the offices, where she realised I'd referred to one Colin and not the other. Suddenly, she believed me that I didn't want the table in my office. "It'll have to stay there," she told me.

New Year is often a time for contemplating life. Too many aggravations from Sueki fell back into my mind; ignoring her around the office no longer sufficed. Under the heading, "*Surplus office items*," I sent the following mail message to all head office staff: "*Dear All, The round table formerly in Colin Z's office and the old safe both sitting in my office both appear to be surplus to requirements of North Sydney (the back up tapes can be kept in the filing cabinet in my office). Please let me know if you know of any other sites that would like them, or if anyone would like to acquire them from the company for their own purposes. Kindest regards, Simon*"

The only time Chris came late to an executive meeting was the morning it seems he sat with Sueki hearing her complain about me. He spoke with Wayne or Greg, before Greg spoke to me. My relationship with Sueki was "poisoning the office," said Greg, although I don't think anyone noticed anything before Sueki complained to Chris.

At a time I thought I could make peace with anyone, I offered to take Sueki out for coffee. She refused.

When I told Wayne I would persevere, he asked me if Sueki and I were going to kiss. He smiled, before asking, "Can I watch?"

Wearing suits and ties at Cement didn't satisfy Wayne. Professional people could, he suggested, wear jackets around the office. (When Wayne said "could" to a fellow executive, he meant "should.") I mentioned his suggestion to Shaun, who recommended I press my shirts. Business shirts should not merely be ironed, but pressed.

Sometimes dressing casually (as he'd dressed that first day I met him) made Chris seem arrogant. Whenever he was meeting directors or other people his equals or superiors, he wore sparkling rich suits and ties.

The next day, I bought a powerful, new steam-pressing iron. The company officially had no dress code, but dress sense.

The simplest and most obvious conformity is in grooming and dress. It was at school, it is everywhere else. Fashion means the conformity changes, but in all cases we abandon our choices to others.

I'd never watched the television series *Big Brother*, but couldn't escape news stories about it. The only memorable line was about a contestant, Gordon I think, along the lines of, "Having a crazy hairstyle can't make up for a beige personality." Some of the freaks might find it difficult to move from a circus to a company office, unless they fix their hair and buy suitable suits.

Each group sets its norms. Norms change.

Wayne suggested the supply chain development manager not smile in meetings, because it lacked "gravitas." He suggested I was "too friendly" at the office. I should be "stand-offish."

Greg didn't share that choice of word, but complained about my "hale and hearty manner." Whatever the words, I was too sociable and cheerful. Greg complained that me asking him if his lunch was "good tucker" was "grating." Head office staff sat silently consuming their food, even when sitting together in the bright kitchen area. I never again asked Greg about the food he sat eating.

None of it changed anything, and I was soon banished far from Sueki to the most distant corner: the office that Colin, the integration manager, said wryly he'd chosen for himself when he established the offices because he wanted to hide. What had been my office became Colin's, where the old safe remained. With me, in my new, much smaller office, was the round table.

Colin had sat facing the window, away from the door. My new office was too thin for my wide desk, but still I twisted the desk around to face the door from the corridor I couldn't see from my chair. Rewiring the electrical, telephone, and computer cabling to make my new space the best I could make it meant the company incurred no end of expenses, but I didn't care. Neither did anyone else.

Sueki secured authority from the information technology division to control the head office electronic address groups, whereby she surreptitiously stripped me from executive access to electronic mail without informing me or anyone else. General managers and I assumed I was still receiving mail directed to executives. It took time to complete but Sueki, a secretary, effectively expunged me from the executive.

My education, qualifications, and skills meant nought, subordinated to an uneducated, incompetent personal assistant of a chief executive otherwise engaged. Amidst my emasculation, I needed some small sense of control. If I imagined walking from that place and never returning, I was imagining forgoing not just that job and income but all others, as every prospective employer would want to know why I'd left. No explanation would make sense, while the truth would unsettle potential employers not wanting to risk aggravation. Nobody hires someone who might upset his or her personal assistant. I wouldn't.

The workplace to which I'd come comfortably before Gary's departure, I came with dread. I could have transferred my car parking space into the building in which we worked when spaces became available, but didn't. Remaining beneath the building across the laneway gave me in my car a little extra distance from the company offices. The lift door opening was like the gates of hell unlocking before me; I grabbed a final breath.

When Sueki stepped into the lift, I said nothing. She too said nothing. When she turned her head away, I smiled.

Jill was one of a few colleagues with whom I conversed in the head office kitchen. Several years older than most other secretaries, she was still much younger than Sueki. Jill was friendly and kind, with a fondness no less for the spirits she perceived from the next world as for people in this. Her cheerfulness, as much as her interest in herbal remedies, matched her wide, flowery dresses. (In much the same way, Sueki matched her thin fitting, dark suits.) "I can't believe the power she has," Jill told me. "If I were you, I'd be looking for another job."

She said essentially the same words several times, before I asked her, "What makes you think that I'm not?"

"Oh," said Jill, unusually falling silent. Her mind rolled through quick, careful thinking before thinking aloud. "I suppose if you were looking for another job, then you wouldn't tell anyone."

Only the partially dismissed Shaun had I trusted enough at head office to say I'd already attended interviews for a job elsewhere. I wasn't particularly attracted to the role bogged down with the minutiae of legal work I'd left behind.

Too individually minded for bravery or heroism, none of the general managers for whom Jill was their secretary defied Sueki's desire to remove her. Nor were they willing to be the one to act against her. Without defensible reason to dismiss her, they hid, while Sueki excluded her from memoranda to other secretaries and allocated her work to Chrissy, a pretty, young secretary with thick, rusty blonde hair. Wanting explanation for what Sueki was doing, Jill approached Wayne in his office. With a candour no one else mustered, Wayne promptly dismissed her.

Jill came to my office to tell me what happened. "Is that legal?" she asked me.

"No," I replied. The company was giving her three months' salary in addition to her accrued leave entitlements. "That's why they're paying you so much money."

Chrissy worked studiously at what had been Jill's desk near the rear door. Displayed unobtrusively on her computer screen was a changing array of photographic images she'd stored there: her with her similarly pretty, young friends, never otherwise seen at the office. They could've been in bars or at parties or been anywhere outdoors, but always their wide mouths seemed to laugh and white teeth seemed to shine. Their arms hung around each other's shoulders, while their free hands held glasses of wine. Chrissy mentioned them when I remarked upon them; her desk was near my secretary's desk. I soon returned to my office. She soon resumed working.

Before she left head office the first Tuesday evening in December 2005, Chrissy informed everyone sitting near the rear door that she'd broken the rear door handle. She might've also affixed a notice beside it.

When Sueki learnt of the broken handle, she asked my fourth secretary to send the following electronic mail message to all head office staff. "*Subject Missing Door Handle – Pacific Hwy Door,*" she headed it. "*Dear All, Please be aware that the internal door handle on the Pacific Highway side of the building is missing. You will need to use the main entrance to leave the office (either via Reception or the door located next to the mailboxes). Building Management has been advised, and the situation will be rectified in the near future. Kind Regards KATRINA…*"

Katrina sent the message at six minutes before six o'clock. Eleven minutes later, Sueki sent a second message to head office staff, headed "*MISSING DOOR HANDLE AT THE WEST WING EXIT DOOR.*" (I'm not sure if she called the Pacific Highway end the West Wing because she thought we were the White House.) Emphasising the seriousness of the issue, her text was emboldened. "*Please note that Chrissy has ripped the door handle off the West Wing exit door without informing EVERYONE of the situation.*

"*Bob…& I only just found out a few minutes ago!*

"*Chrissy, This a potential safety issue. There is now* NO EXIT *from that area.*

"*Have you organised for Gianni to come fix the handle immediately?*

"*If not, call them first thing tomorrow morning when you arrive to the office & let me know what's being organised.*

"*Please be aware of your responsibility in this office & keep us informed of any safety impediments around the office. Rgds Sueki*"

Five minutes later, Sueki sent a third message, this one headed "*MISSING DOOR HANDLE AT THE WEST WING EXIT DOOR – Follow up.*" As well as being emboldened, this message qualified for a bright blue font, adding to the fray. "*I just spoke to Gianni, our resident handyman & stressed the importance of getting the door handle fixed due to no exit from the West Wing. Gianni will come by tonite to rectify the matter. Rgds Sueki"* (A broken door handle mattered more to Sueki than spelling or grammar.)

At thirteen minutes before nine o'clock in the morning, Gisella responded, suitably chastened. *"Good morning all, I apologise for not informing North Sydney staff of the following;*

"– Chrissy came to see me about the door handle as soon as it happened ~ 4:15pm

"– Paul…also informed me about the door handle ~ 4:20pm

"– I called Gianni at ~ 4:22pm about the door handle.

"– Gianni advised me that he will be in that night to fix the door handle. He asked me to leave the broken door handle on my desk, for him to repair.

"– I informed Paul and Chrissy that Gianni will be in that night to repair it.

"I apologise for not informing all North Sydney users. Kind regards, Gisella…"

The rest of head office staff quietly read the saga across our computer screens. To participate would've made us lunatics too, if we weren't lunatics already.

An hour and a half later, possibly feeling wounded, Chrissy sheepishly sent a message to all head office staff. *"Just popping out to buy some new glasses for the office – we are running a bit short."*

A few months later, after securing a job elsewhere, Chrissy escaped altogether. Corporations are the only asylums that impose more tests upon people before admitting them, than before letting them flee.

11

Total Commitment to Work

While I was a student at senior school, an older boys' magazine recorded the headmaster telling them, "I am still the headmaster when I take my clothes off." He didn't demonstrate the point.

No longer are people in jobs only while performing those functions, like we're pedestrians only when crossing the road. We're never unemployed, but between positions or consulting. Not merely the means of earning money, work became our identity. It's all we see when we look in the mirror and all we feel when we lie in our beds in the darkness of night. It affirms, defines, and becomes us.

Private schools were exempt from New South Wales laws prohibiting mandatory retirement ages and other discrimination. Many years after I'd left and after nearly three decades in the role, the headmaster reached sixty-five years of age. Wanting a change, the school council compelled him to leave. Nothing could compel him to retire. After departing that Uniting Church school, for two years he consulted across the city in Bondi to Yeshiva, a Jewish college. From there, he became headmaster of King Abdul Aziz, a Muslim college in another corner of Sydney, Rooty Hill. Where he worked or the children mattered less than him remaining a headmaster or consulting close to it.

Employers like employees ingrained in their work. Consternation seethed through my former school when the new, younger headmaster chose not to live in the headmaster's official residence between the main iron gates and sciences block within the school grounds. Neither would any subsequent headmaster live in the school: he demolished the ages-old cottage. At a school where headmasters' tenures could often be counted in decades, his lasted five years.

Our real guiding principles become comply, conform, and commit; that third C distinguishes our postmodern West from everything else. The commitment isn't to spouses, families, countries, or God, but to work.

Successful people aren't those for whom work is merely an adjunct to life. They're those committed completely to their careers. Michael, the senior taxation partner at the first law firm in which I worked after being admitted as a solicitor, reputedly sat up in bed dictating memoranda into a small cassette tape recorder, while his wife lay beside him.

We take ourselves seriously. A criminal barrister (that is to say, a barrister at the criminal bar, acting in criminal matters) friend of mine asked an instructing solicitor why she'd mailed him a joke. Phil S meant to be rude; humour doesn't intrude upon labour. She didn't send him another. He told me the story.

A year or so before joining Cement Australia, I attended a dinner party in Oxford Falls. "It would be awful," I remarked to a Canadian mother of two, "if a career got in the way of parenthood."

"It would be awful," replied Nancy, "if parenthood got in the way of a career."

My friend Kathryn D was a charmingly sociable partner of a midsized law firm. Around about the time I left Cement, a colleague of hers told me she sent mail messages from her palm organiser three hours after her baby's birth.

Over lunch, my friend Rehana mentioned having read of a lawyer at that firm who attended a property settlement wearing her hospital wristband, before racing back to her hospital bed. It might've had nothing to do with childbirth.

During one of my two visits to Cement's old offices for interviews before being awarded the job there, I saw Greg headed to a photocopier. Exuding comfort without show, I was surprised to see so many shades of grey in one person: his hair and moustache, shirt, woollen ties, and trousers. They made him likeable, natural, unfazed by fashions that had become more boring than grey ever was.

Having been Gary's counterpart in the southern premerger company as well as its company secretary, business analyst, and almost everything else he could do at a desk, Greg meticulously researched matters in what he called his bailiwick. He was second only to Gary in patiently briefing me in my new role, as well as joining Gary and me the Friday evening we secretly opened a bottle of red wine in the boardroom. Married to a Japanese woman he'd met in Japan after studying Japanese in Australia, he'd been a scoutmaster when their son was young and active at the government schools when their two children were pupils there. His wife I knew because she'd come to the first Cement Christmas party. He only mentioned his family when I asked about them.

I asked about families a lot, but conversations about our weekends or Australian football I'd made with Gary each Monday morning were strained encounters with Greg, as if I were wasting his time by asking. I soon stopped asking. Greg worked and talked: talked about work. The communications manageress described him as "the world's most boring man."

(I liked that about Greg. I liked the communications manageress for not being boring.)

Every Sunday, equipped with a packed lunch brought from home because the nearby food courts were closed, Greg sat in his office. Particularly on Sundays, he distributed memoranda often no more than him thinking in type, imparting his ideas for work. (Greg didn't use words like "memoranda." He asked me to change "*fora*" to "*forums*" in one memorandum I wrote and insurance "*premiums*" in place of "*premia*" in another, while acknowledging I'd been correct.) I'd updated Ron's electronic table of subsidiary and associated companies and major investments whenever they changed, but never had the time or thought for doing anything more. One Sunday, Greg carefully reformatted the table with beautiful colours and shades.

Chris often told employees, "I don't expect you to work *every* weekend." The implication was clear: time away from work was merely respite. (To his credit, Chris seemed never to have attended the office on weekends.) He complained of the Brisbane office to a Cement executive meeting that "you wouldn't want to be caught in the rush to the lifts at Milton at five o'clock."

Greg said office hours began at nine o'clock in the morning. Wayne said the "in crowd" arrived at eight o'clock. Greg wasn't part of that crowd. He arrived before seven, eating breakfast in the office eating area after his morning swim. He was also the last to leave the offices each evening; the light near his corner of the floor shone conspicuously, when everything else was dark.

During my annual performance review in my far-corner office early in 2005, Greg made one brief mention of Sueki. I criticised her small mindedness. He didn't mention her again. Without issue with my work, his only criticism of me was what he called the "perception" I was "swanning around." (Greg always spoke in the third person, describing his wife as "the wife," his children as "the son" and "the daughter," and his mother-in-law as "the mother-in-law," so I assumed he was talking about his perception. Then again, he also did what he was told. The perception might have been Sueki's, relayed to him.)

"What?" I responded. "Do you mean the way I walk?"

"No, no," he said hurriedly. Greg went onto complain of me as the other two past executives of the southern premerger company, Colin and Shaun, had complained of employees at the northern premerger company: that when we travelled, we flew during what Greg called "gentlemanly hours." We boarded aircraft to arrive before scheduled meetings began, instead of setting forth before sunrise and expending whole days at our destinations scrounging about for new tasks. While those northern premerger company employees and I returned home when our meetings were finished, Greg, Colin, and Shaun returned home late at night.

Thereafter, I booked my flights for early mornings and evenings. They were accordingly entered into my electronic diary, which Joanna had told me Sueki checked. I then quietly changed the bookings to my gentlemanly hours, without amending my diary. Cement paid the fees.

The challenge for employees becomes not letting the company know what the company oughtn't to know, but confiding in the company monitors whatever we'd like the company to think. Free market economics is predicated on individual self-interest.

Greg also went onto complain, in that performance review, "You enjoy lunches and dinners too much."

They're the leisure that employment can bring, although the only corporate entertainment I'd attended during working hours was a Melbourne Cup function at the CBD Hotel as a guest of Wayne's employment lawyer. With me were the plant and people performance manager and knowledge and capability manager, but most products of the human resources division were anathemas to Greg, Colin, and Shaun. We drank beer and wine, especially Champagne. We wore hats and exotic ties. Some guests smoked cigars. "I enjoy meeting people," I told Greg.

"But not to the exclusion of work."

Unlike Gary a year earlier, Greg had declined the insurance broker's invitation to fly him and me (and our wives) to the Formula One Grand Prix in Melbourne. Instead, Greg spent that Sunday, like all other Sundays, in the office.

Corporate hospitality had become slothfulness, unless it's a chance to further business objectives. Greg did leave the office early one Sunday to come to a cricket match in Sydney as a guest of a bank; his work involved banking more than insurance. Watching the cricket, he talked about work.

The annual Cement golf days were customer marketing with Col responsible. (I imagine they'd been leisure when Shaun was in charge.) Greg never considered participating in them, and frowned when I attended a dinner afterwards. (I'd never become sufficiently passionate about business to learn to play golf.)

No longer did I invite Greg to the rare mining industry lunches I attended, having regard to the coal mines within his bailiwick. Corporate inhospitality at the office made corporate hospitality elsewhere more important, but I ceased recording corporate entertainment in my electronic diary. I simply scheduled meetings from twelve thirty to one o'clock, in the insurance broker's offices.

Come the next Melbourne Cup, I slipped away sometime after two o'clock to join the same two human resources managers at the CBD Hotel that I'd joined there a year earlier. Again we ate and drank, and I met people I'd have never otherwise met. Wayne eventually joined us, after attending another function with Chris as guests of a recruitment agency. (Cement could well have been the agency's best client.) The next morning, Greg chided me for not informing my secretary I would not return to the office that afternoon. (That was to say, for not having entered the function in my electronic diary where Sueki could see it. Greg rarely came looking for me.)

"You could have called me on my mobile," I replied.

He muttered, "There was nothing that important."

I'd continued with my private career. The Lexis Nexus publishing company invited me to present a paper about insurance and indemnity clauses to a procurement contracts conference in Brisbane in August 2005. Before I could go, I needed to convince Greg that my afternoon away from work would "add value" not to anyone attending the conference or me but Cement.

With hindsight, that could have been my fault. I'd led the efforts to include "*I add value to the business in everything I do*" among the five guiding principles. Only Greg paid attention to them.

The benefits to Cement of me speaking at a procurement conference weren't obvious, but my profession was to argue cases that weren't immediately obvious. The days I spent preparing my paper were the only times I came to the office on weekends since Sueki banished me to my corner room.

Appearing an unlikely combination, the two Cement procurement officers – stocky Stuart much older than I was and Catherine a few years younger – seemed to spend all their time together. "As long as your wife doesn't mind," I joked, as we stood together on a balcony between sessions of the second leadership conference.

"Catherine is my wife," responded Stuart (his second wife, to be precise). They'd met at one workplace and came to the northern premerger company together, before setting off together to that company's Swiss owner (Cement's Swiss shareholder). He had two children, I think, from his first marriage.

Stuart went onto tell me the mistake wasn't just mine. At one procurement conference, there was great surprise when attendees saw one of them leaving the other's hotel room.

I invited them to lunch one day I was in Brisbane because Catherine was an occasional poetess (although poetry didn't add value to the company business). Part way through a master's university course when they arrived at Cement, she'd not asked the company to pay her course costs or sought to interrupt her working hours to study. She just wanted company work not to intrude upon her evenings and weekends when she studied and to take her holiday leave when examinations were scheduled.

John, the manufacturing general manager whose responsibilities at the time encompassed procurement, allowed her no leeway. "You'll be too busy," he told her. Catherine withdrew from her course.

The company wouldn't indulge what Wayne called "course junkies." Presumably, the prestigious and costly managerial course Chris later approved the company paying for him to attend in France didn't make him an addict.

While inertia from the past still had some influence soon after I'd joined Cement, the company conducted a cement industry course lasting several days in Gladstone. (The northern premerger company had conducted it once or twice a year.) I hadn't needed Gary's approval to attend, but he saw the benefit in me attending. An executive committee meeting scheduled at the same time required me to defer my attendance.

With Wayne's human resources division focussed upon visions, values, and films, the company didn't convene another course for almost two years. Several months before it was due to be held, in October that year, I told Greg I planned to attend. The course would assist me in dealing with product liability claims and broaden my scientific and commercial knowledge.

When I came to enrol and company procedures had come to require me to get Greg's approval, he refused. He'd never undertaken such a course, he said, as if that were a reason I shouldn't.

Greg never seemed more confining and narrow than when he explained that I would be too busy working on the two projects he'd listed in my performance objectives for the year, on which ten percent of my annual monetary bonus depended. They weren't the grand and glorious compliance programmes or even the abstract broadening of the legal role I'd agreed with Gary. Instead, one was an electronic document register. The other I can't recall. Describing them in Colin's computer system for such projects, I needed to quantify their monetary values to the company: nil, nil.

Greg called them SMARTA objectives, having learnt the acronym at the company from which he was still officially seconded: specific, measurable, achievable, results orientated, time orientated, and agreed. (Greg mightn't have liked courses, but he loved acronyms.) However much Greg held in disdain the extravagant pursuits of the Cement human resources department, he stood devoted to anything from the company that for three decades employed him.

I wouldn't have minded so much if I'd thought Greg fretted about my failing to complete those tasks affecting his bonus (although plenty of time remained in the year for me to complete them). Greg didn't think like that. Work was important to him for its own sake.

I stormed back to my far end of the offices, where I vented my frustration with words the knowledge and capability manager never before heard me use. I expected Paul McN to report the substance if not every detail of my comments to Wayne. Perhaps he didn't.

So livid was I with Greg, I sought his permission to attend the annual Australian Corporate Lawyers Association conference in Melbourne so he'd refuse me. Better than that, he approved me going. It related to work.

12

Economy without Empathy

In one of my more melancholy moments of youth, I wrote a short song around the chorus, "*Nobody cares if you live or die just so long as you get your work done.*" One line was, "*Nobody cares if you're here or there, or everywhere, just so long as you get your work done.*" I could have elaborated by writing something like, "*Nobody cares if you're a complete raving lunatic just so long as you espouse our vision and values.*" Being a complete raving lunatic probably helps.

A partner at one medium-sized law firm tossed Paddle Pop ice creams to his colleagues. At least he related with people.

Among my Cement Australia colleagues to whom I told the reason I'd been sent to my new corner office was the packaged products general manager. I'd first met Peter M more than a year earlier, in the poor light of a Wiseman's Ferry hotel gazebo when he was among the managers invited to brief the executives before we drafted the new company's values, although we'd often spoken by telephone before then. Like me, he was an executive for some purposes but not others. In spite of six years in his role, he felt that when first they met, Chris didn't like him. Chris wouldn't, for Peter had flair in his stride, spoke of imagination in marketing, and came to speak freely, at least with me, of his feelings. (I can't imagine Peter having worked on his car.)

Working hard and well but still being pushed aside affected people with feelings as it didn't affect people without them, although people without them seemed less likely to be pushed aside anyway. Soon after Chris empowered Sueki to knobble me, Peter told me, referring to Chris and Wayne, "I'm worried they're trying to get rid of me."

"Peter," I responded, "I'm far more worried that they're not" trying to get rid of *me*.

Whether Chris and Wayne were in Melbourne the afternoon before Easter anyway or made the trip for that purpose, they dismissed Peter. Martin added packaged products to his growing portfolio.

For his part, Peter complained to me about the time it was done, with every management expert saying people should be dismissed early in a week and never before holidays. For my part, I'd long stopped expecting correlation between what management experts professed and what managers did (not simply at Cement). Chris and Wayne dismissed Peter when best not for Peter, but for them.

Peter dealt with his dismissal the way we'd learnt to deal with adversity. He told me a year later, as I prepared to leave Cement, that he always felt better about anything after buying a new shirt.

Wayne and the safety, health, environment, and quality general manager Bob wanted Cement to perform periodic medical examinations of employees. Addressing the executive committee meeting the third Friday in May 2005, Chris insisted the company pay only for examinations warranted by the "risk matrix" it faced in a particular person being sick or dying. (Rarely has human life seemed more trivial than it did being called part of a risk matrix.) If employees wanted medical tests, we could pay for them. "We're not doing it because we care."

Management had moved far from the paternalistic old days of the much-maligned (by people who'd not worked there) northern premerger company. Gary, long after his dismissal, told me it arranged medical examinations for its employees because it did care.

Gary and I were sharing lunch in Brisbane with Ron and Kaye. Gary and his wife had retired to Noosa, playing golf and tennis, but when he wanted to pay for his meal I insisted the company pay. "I know it all worked out well for you," I told him, "but I don't think you were treated with respect."

Respecting people was one of Cement's guiding principles. Gary put his wallet away.

Companies sometimes retrench employees because they no longer require them, without fault on their part. Australian companies generally pay redundant employees periods of salary, often linked to the length of time they've been employed. Each time the Cement executive considered a new redundancy policy, Chris checked that the policy didn't apply to him or other executives around the table, whose contracts of employment determined their entitlements. Executives then set about reducing employee entitlements to the minimum levels they could, without spurring an employee exodus. That's the free market.

I, in my previous naïvety, hadn't included a redundancy entitlement in my contract. Wayne mentioned that his contract entitled him to six months' salary, after Chris refused him anything more. That seemed to be the amount in all the new general manager contracts. In every conversation I could with Wayne, I mentioned that I would never accept anything less than six months' salary, were I made redundant.

In early December 2004, the general manager of a Cement joint venture told a joint venture board meeting of his plans to retrench several redundant employees. When Don mentioned deferring their retrenchment until after Christmas, a joint venture director (nominated not by Cement but by the other investor) asked, "Why?"

A young man with a family, Don struggled to find words to explain what he'd presumed didn't need explanation. The director might've been making a point, or might've not understood any significance of Christmas for employees and their families. In either event, no other director spoke up (although Shaun suggested to me later he'd been taken aback). I, the meagre company secretary, simply took note. I took lots of notes.

Don was seconded to that joint venture from Cement, to which Wayne told me Don would never return. Chris gave Don written notice of his failings (other than those related to not wanting to fire people before Christmas) and time to correct them, as the law required, before firing him six months later.

Being reluctant to fire people showed a lack of leadership, Wayne once told the supply chain development manager. There was no end of leadership at Cement.

Wayne's list of employees marked for expulsion forever found new names to replace those of people expelled. Economic theory presumes that company executives want to maximise company profit, but those dismissals cost the company expertise, accumulated knowledge, and a small country's economy worth of termination payments and recruitment costs hiring their replacements. Profit maximisation is selective: a reason not to keep people, but to pay lesser people less money when they go.

No real company interest was behind the long litany of wanton dismissals. There were only individual interests, but not those of people departing or their families.

Many years earlier, before the formation of Cement and coming of Chris, management and the board of the northern premerger company wanted to convert an old kiln to produce lime, but the returns wouldn't warrant spending the thirty million dollars they knew it would cost. In order to justify the project proceeding to their Swiss shareholder, they officially estimated the cost to be only twenty-five million dollars.

Their plan, when the additional five million dollars in costs unfolded, was to find reasons beyond their control for the increase.

Responsible for managing the project was Mal, a pleasant, inoffensive fellow who conversed freely when spoken to but was unlikely to initiate conversations. An engineer, he'd been with the company for thirty-one years.

In the new world of Cement, Chris pressed everyone for plans to improve profitability. An engineer by training, Chris analysed every proposal, approving only what was financially prudent. He considered his approval a personal contract between him and the proponent, for which the proponent was accountable. Costs running over budget by five million dollars would be gross incompetence.

Chris and Wayne wanted to remove Mal for being part of the old company culture, but Mal's employment contract guaranteed him a redundancy payment of one month's salary for each year of service. Including two years with Cement, Mal would be entitled to thirty-three months' salary if the company made him redundant. Thus, Wayne proudly informed executives that he was restructuring the strategy and projects division to offer Mal a new role of "equivalent nature" to his current role, so there would be no redundancy. Confident that Mal would fail in his new role, the company could then dismiss him for poor performance upon three months' notice.

Colin, as strategy and projects general manager, insisted the role be truly equivalent and that Mal have a chance to succeed. A few other executives agreed. The normally combative Wayne just nodded, as if Colin's demands were already part of his plan.

Quietly after the meeting, I told Wayne I hoped he'd consulted with his employment lawyer about what he was planning to do, because he was "sailing pretty close to the wind." I had no power to do anything more.

Wise to what was happening, Mal asked a friend with whom he'd worked at the northern premerger company, by then a director appointed by the Swiss shareholder, for help. Chris' individual self-interest would surely have made him defer to a director's intervention, but the director's response to Mal was a cursory assurance to Chris he wouldn't intervene. Such is friendship in the individualist West.

Colin hadn't seemed to mind Mal approaching a director, but was furious when Mal consulted a lawyer. Mal didn't receive any remuneration increase with his annual performance review letter that year, although he did have his offer of a new role. Mal wrote to Colin declining that role (in a letter most likely drafted by his lawyer), adding obliquely that he expected Cement to "*do the right thing*." Colin presented Mal's letter to the April executive committee meeting.

Executives were aghast. "It's all about the money," growled Colin, earning many times more money than Mal earned. Like Chris and the other general managers sitting around him at the table, Colin also enjoyed uncapped annual bonuses. Their bonuses that year would add more than sixty percent to their annual remunerations. In the offing was an additional Long Term Incentive Scheme available only to executives. "I don't want someone working for me who's only doing it for the money."

The normally amiable Martin insisted Mal's letter was effectively his resignation. (He, perhaps also Greg, mightn't always feel certain of what he said about Mal as he was that day. Inside company meeting rooms, where profits obscure all other perspectives and executives focus so well on their jobs, even the kindest of people can come to be callous.)

"I wouldn't pay him," said Col.

Greg agreed. Executives who'd previously insisted Mal be offered a truly equivalent role and have a chance to succeed, abandoned him.

Chris became angry, complaining of Mal, "He's causing a lot of distress around this table." The financial impact on Chris and the general managers (and other employees) was a small portion of their annual bonuses. The impact upon Mal, not quite near enough retirement age, and his family was four hundred thousand dollars. "Get him here," cried Chris, "and tell him he can have fifty thousand dollars to sign a deed of release, or he can take us to court!"

The distress of executives passed within minutes, as we proceeded through the rest of the meeting agenda. That night, we enjoyed our executive dinners with wine. Mal and his family's distress would dog them for at least as long as Mal fought the company.

Mal said he was suing Cement for unfair dismissal in a job interview with Cement's principal competitor, which promptly informed Wayne. Job applicants can't say anything worse to prospective employers than that they're suing their last employers. The best course is to secure their new job and then sue.

The central executive clique decided Cement would file every possible motion and contest every issue so Mal incurred costs in response, however likely the company was to lose. Whatever the outcome in law and however much money the company spent (even if more money than Mal was demanding), Mal was to earn no profit from his action. The company was punishing Mal, but also warning what Chris (or possibly Wayne) told an executive committee meeting were the "five or six other employees lined up" to take the same course of action as Mal because they didn't like where Chris had taken the company. They were surely names on Wayne's perennial list.

After one meeting, perhaps the one at which Wayne told the employment lawyer to do all he could to impose costs upon Mal whatever the cost to the company, Colin told the employment lawyer and me about a conversation he'd had with an employee from Cement's principal competitor. The employee had asked Wayne, "What do you do?"

Wayne replied, "I f**k with people's lives."

We do what we need to do to alleviate duress, as best as we can. We do nothing more. Bullying elicits meagre obedience. When people putting their heads up find their faces slapped around often enough, they learn to lie low. That's self-interest. We nod, we smile, but we don't imagine and don't create.

Otter and Cement both offered anonymous counselling services for their employees; friends are for people who don't have careers. (As my friend Barry pointed out and as Chris' friend Martin and Greg's friend Bruce typified, the friends for people who do have careers are consultants.) Professional counsellors do as they're told, without difficult vagaries or unpleasant compromise. Unlike friends, they remain, for as long as somebody pays: the best of friends.

Among the multitude of companies counselling other companies' employees was one that employed my Hong Kong Chinese friend Ted, a psychologist. (To be such friends again, Ted and I must've not had careers anymore.) Counselling Ted about his awful work conditions dominated a telephone conversation between us lasting one hundred and eight minutes, the second Wednesday of August, 2007. Unfortunately, Ted's employer hadn't hired me to counsel its employees.

No employee was more naïve than Ted. He thought he should tell his manager that the long working hours, stress, and other appalling work conditions within the counselling service caused its high turnover of staff. I assured him that whatever Ted observed in his short time working there, his manager already knew. Telling the manager would have treated him like an idiot. It might also have sounded like Ted threatening to leave, involving the manager's ego.

The employee counselling service didn't need to provide its employees with counselling services. New counsellors kept coming, work was being done, and profits were higher than they would've been had money been spent to improve working conditions. Hell, the counselling service had bought a microwave oven for the kitchen. That ought to compensate for a few more hours working each day.

Money can't alleviate every distress. Never able to understand why she'd been dismissed from Cement, Jill spent several months in professional counselling. No longer an employee, it was her expense.

13

Parenthood by Stealth

Researchers from Clark University and the Centre for Creative Leadership in Greensboro, North Carolina, reported in 2007 that employees with families perform best in the office and parents make the best managers. So, what? Employers no longer want the best performers and managers. We want the most committed. Commitment makes someone best.

As long ago as 1987, at the second law firm at which I worked after my admission as a solicitor, a senior associate popped into the offices after the birth of his child. A female partner didn't think to congratulate the commercial lawyer or his wife for the birth or recognise his diligence for being there that day. Instead, she berated him for wearing casual clothes to the office.

Even the Holyman finance director Reuben, a loving father of three, referred to my baby son as "the grommet." I didn't respond. At the time, I was begging his and Griff's permission to convert my business-class airfare to three economy-class fares for my wife and son to accompany me on a long business trip to Europe.

Western children are no longer born to their race and nations (as those of other races and nations remain born to theirs), but to individuals. No longer are we societies embracing those children as our own. We don't support each other giving birth, their children, or the fathers of their children. We don't support them beforehand or afterwards, beyond what we must.

The second Cement Australia internal auditor was at first pleased when Greg (to whom he reported) sent his wife flowers, after he explained he needed to work from home for a few days because she'd miscarried what would've been their first child. After returning to the office, Stuart D told Greg approaching him at his desk, "I wanted to thank you personally for the flowers."

"It's expected," Greg replied, before quickly proceeding to talk about work.

Greg was a good, well-meaning man, without vices I saw and honest almost to a fault, but managers well versed in work and company values don't need proficiency in human sensitivities. We lost interest in them, beyond what's expected.

When my third daughter was born, some of my colleagues, including Shaun, telephoned me. Greg didn't. Nor did he remark when I came to the office for the executive committee meeting the next day. (Employment was too insecure at Cement and I was still too financially insecure to risk taking the five days' paternity leave to which company policy nominally entitled me. Given that was the meeting at which Chris announced Shaun's constructive dismissal, it was probably just as well that I came.) During a break, Greg muttered to me, "I suppose I better congratulate you on the birth of your child."

Etiquette fulfilled, Greg never initiated conversation about my children again. Even if I tried to initiate a conversation about them, I'm not sure he ever reciprocated.

The human traits we've become unwilling to touch aren't just those involved with the beginning of life, but also the end. Having heard Colin was suddenly headed back to South Africa (the sanctuary for white former Rhodesians and Zimbabweans) because his father was dying, I gave him my sympathies, in a short uneasy conversation between us in the kitchen. I don't think my words meant anything.

I missed a sales and operations planning meeting one Monday morning to take a long telephone call from my wife because, as I told Bruce, half a day earlier in a river in France, my brother-in-law drowned. No etiquette required anyone around the office to say anything to me. Only with Anna, a company accountant based in Melbourne, did we sit in a bar at Park Road in Milton honouring Bill with glasses of Armagnac. Sometime earlier, Anna told me I was the only person who made her feel welcome when she first visited head office.

Soon afterwards, Anna raised Wayne's ire by bailing up a human resources employee saying she wanted a career path in the company, as he told me in a conversation in his office. She'd assumed the human resources department was there to serve employees. She swiftly disappeared.

The first people I met who ate meat pies with knives and forks (as I came to do, as I aged) were Cement executives, when served them for lunch during daylong executive meetings. Meals without meat or other animal products were always provided for John, the manufacturing general manager. At dinner the first night at the Retreat

Hotel restaurant, during our Wiseman's Ferry retreat drafting the new company's guiding principles, John's meal was conspicuously different to others. "Why?" I asked him.

John didn't trumpet being a vegan (he didn't trumpet anything), or eat with an ideological viewpoint. He simply ate as he'd eaten since he was young, saying he felt better and believed he was healthier not eating animal products. (I learnt a lot of my colleagues from talking to them about matters other than work.)

In a much later conversation more about work, where no one else heard us, John succinctly summarised the Cement culture by quoting managers more confident talking to him than confiding in other executives. "Do what you're told, or you're fired!" (They should've been charged with drafting the guiding principles.)

Employees mistrusted anyone from the human resources department, especially those Wayne positioned within their divisions. John expected his plant and people performance manager to report everything John said and did back to Wayne.

Beginning at eight o'clock in the morning and scheduled to finish at five o'clock in the afternoon (with times marked for each agenda item to finish), the monthly executive committee meetings increasingly dragged into the evenings. So, Chris convened his dinners the previous night. When Chris' other commitments prevented him from hosting a dinner, I quietly left the dinners off subsequent meeting agendas; Glen Thomas and Bob were no less pleased than I was. After a few months' respite, Chris restored them.

John's family had remained in Brisbane when the merger forming Cement led him (like Gary) to take lodgings in Sydney. Organising his work around Brisbane, John was able to move back there, flying to Sydney when meetings required it. (John impressed Gary no end that he did.)

To attend the executive dinners scheduled the night before the committee meetings, John would've needed to come to Sydney a day earlier than he came just for the meetings. What so powerfully reflected the schism between him and Chris wasn't John being a vegan or so gently spoken as he was, but John citing undefined commitments to his family in Brisbane as his reason for not attending the dinners. Even when the executive committee met in Brisbane and dinner was there, John remained with his family. Married with three teenage children, John knew his job was secure because of the record production levels from his manufacturing division. He went so far as to order an expensive new boat for his weekends.

Chris fired him because, he told John, he wanted the manufacturing division to increase its use of alternative fuel resources, such as worn tyres, in its kilns. The reason was plainly untrue. (Chris didn't need to fire anyone to alter what the company fed into its kilns.)

When first we'd met, my third secretary at Cement grinned with a smile as large as she was, talking about life away from her job. I didn't know what a grip on a film set was, in spite of seeing the job mentioned in the closing credits to films, before Joanna explained; her husband was one. Two years later, she scowled as well as any company employee interrupted from the tasks for which she sat intensely at her desk. (I hope that wasn't because of me.)

Many months earlier, she'd been cited in the 'Diversity in Action' article in the sixth edition of the *Vision* magazine. Pregnant with twins, Joanna supposedly exemplified the company's flexible working arrangements for mothers, although the article omitted to mention her failed attempts to use her accrued holiday leave every Wednesday leading up to her maternity leave. Sueki complained to the receptionist, Gisella, "We might as well *all* have babies!"

Where compliance matters so much, babies can be singularly non-compliant. Sueki had refused to countenance any flexible working arrangements for Joanna after she returned from maternity leave, before it seems Wayne coaxed her into complying with the law. Presumably, he already wanted Joanna for that upcoming edition of *Vision*.

Most people were unaware that the legal requirement for employers to provide three months' paid maternity leave didn't mean three months *after* the birth of a child, until Joanna wanted to begin her leave one month before the due date of birth. If her babies remained within her beyond their full term, she would receive less than two months' paid leave after birth. The company honoured the strict letter of its legal obligations, nothing more.

Away from the *Vision* magazine, babies and children were unmentionables. Amidst the ruckus from Sueki after I tried to remove surplus furniture from my office, Greg asked me, "Can you think of any other times you've upset her?"

"No," I said, shaking my head.

"Think again."

Slowly, I remembered. "She was upset about my email selling ballet school chocolates."

Greg began nodding. Six months earlier, I'd sent the following message to all head office staff, concerning my two elder daughters.

"Esther and Rosie's ballet school is having a fund raising, selling the lovely chocolate bars outside my office for just (yes, just) $2 each. They and I thank them for any support you can give. Cheers, Simon" I then walked from my office.

"You should have consulted me first," Sueki barked. "It was totally unprofessional. People in this office are much too busy to worry about your children's fundraising."

The box of chocolates was soon back on my desk. One bar was missing, not paid for.

Other employees (including Wayne) had happily bought bars unaware of her reaction. They might've simply liked chocolate.

Discussing that incident six months later with Greg was surreal, but everything at that office had become surreal. "I never did it again," I told him, "even though the children have other fundraising activities."

"Sueki didn't know you wouldn't do it again," he explained. "She thinks you weren't respecting her position. I know you weren't obliged to, but you should have told her that you accepted her position and would not do it again."

Greg went onto say Sueki also felt pressured by me more than a year earlier, soon after the company moved into the spacious new head office. I'd suggested we buy a birthday cake for Gary. Dragana, my first secretary, wouldn't dare do so without Sueki's approval. So, I suggested to Sueki the company buy cakes to celebrate birthdays for each of the fifteen or so employees at head office. There might have been one cake, for Bob's birthday, before Joanna told me Sueki and Greg said there'd be no more. I didn't mention the idea again.

A year later, being reminded by Greg of my meek suggestion, I shook my head. I shrugged my shoulders. Throwing my arms in the air, I lamented, "We're talking about ballet chocolates and birthday cake!"

Trying to placate Sueki soon after the ballet school chocolates, I'd asked her about bringing my two-month-old baby daughter to the office Christmas party. Foolishly, so many years since I last tried to bring a baby to a company function, I'd expected no issue. Asking her was meant to make her fell important, even magnanimous, allowing it.

"No," replied Sueki.

"Alicia is breastfeeding," I explained. "That means she can't come."

"Bring someone else."

"I could bring Esther."

"No children."

My wife was distressed about being compelled to store milk or be excluded from the Cement party; she'd kindly sent a card of gratitude after the company sent her flowers on the birth of our child (as was expected). She wouldn't attend the Christmas party at all.

After much deliberating, I too declined to attend, unwilling to socialise while my wife and our baby daughter were confined to home. At a private lunch we shared many months later, Gary described my action as a "career-limiting move." A lot of moves were career limiting at Cement.

No less career limiting, as it turned out, I'd stopped bothering Sueki with the smiles and greetings I accorded most people. I was never as curt with her as she was with everyone but Chris, but that wasn't the point. Western individualism erases every loyalty except those that corporate individualism demands: to more powerful managers. Familial loyalty is incompatible with company values.

Sitting in his office, Wayne said later he supported Sueki's decision not to allow our child on the boat, although he supported almost all her decisions. He claimed she'd consulted with him, but her reply to me had been immediate; any consultation with Wayne could have only been afterwards. "We would have felt terrible if anything had happened," Wayne told me.

"You'd have got over it."

If I didn't point him to the photographs of his parents on his office window shelf, I should've done. Worse than my loyalty was my emotion, choking in my throat as I told Wayne of the wrong that was the exclusion of anyone's children, not mine alone. There's no place in our corporate, postmodern, individualist West for a man to love or care for another person, not even his wife or baby.

Presumably sensing the legal risks he'd been taking, or possibly just marketing himself, Wayne told me the company "was sympathetic to the demands of your six children." Whatever that meant, it didn't mean letting them upset the chief executive's personal assistant. All it really meant was sometimes working from home or slipping late into the offices or early away from them, although other employees did the same for many childless reasons: attending appointments, buying coffee and croissants.

Instead of resigning after accepting a job offer elsewhere, I imagined Cement offering me money to leave immediately. (Corporate fiefdoms can be useful as much for the serfs as the masters and mistresses.) All I needed to do was send a message around head office selling chocolates for my children's school.

My mother sometimes reprimanded her raucous children by saying,

"Children should be seen and not heard." Many a Western businessman or woman expects children not to be seen, heard, or mentioned.

Wrongful life is a legal action brought on behalf of a child who allegedly should never have been born, but was born because of a doctor or other person's negligence. Punishing parenthood makes any child impinging upon an adult a wrongful life.

Long after she'd resigned, Kathryn, that young Brisbane accounts clerk, told me Cement replaced her job with three jobs. A woman scheduled for an interview for one of those three jobs contacted Kaye, the group accountant, to say she was running late because her child was sick. The normally friendly Kaye told the woman to forget the interview altogether.

We learn to keep children secret if we want to remain employed. Working parents left their children too sick for school for the day in the Myer department store toy section, Charlestown, at which my mother-in-law worked, but not because my mother-in-law was nearby.

Maureen, a board member of a charity counselling children in our local municipality, told me of children who suffered because their wealthy parents worked sixteen hours a day with the aid of cocaine. (Company values don't care about that.) Those upturned noses proved hollow.

14

Managing Expectations

At Cement Australia, I did what I told Chris I would do that first time we met: my job as well as anyone could do it. I considered each way the two premerger companies did anything and chose the better of the two or another way even better, in my view. (That included the document register.) Rarely did I pepper my conversations with talk of vision, guiding principles, or branding, not to promulgate them anyway.

What remained were my small insurrections. Andrew and I learnt we'd attended the same school, although he was a few years younger than I was and we'd not known each other then. That common background might've given us confidence to brave our impressions of Cement, across headrests in a bus on our way to an airport after one conference. In the darkness where no one else could hear, I spoke of the people who'd addressed the conference bearing their personal testaments to the guiding principles in their lives. Andrew responded, "I was trying not to vomit."

"Managing expectations," was probably Chris' favourite phrase. For him as chief executive, the important expectations were those of the three Cement shareholders. Those shareholders also had shareholders, for whom they managed expectations.

In preparing the 2004 accounts, which were already horrific, Chris instructed general managers to be generous in their provisions for future costs and expenses. Any amount by which actual costs and expenses in 2005 fell short of those provisions would become profit in 2005. Conversely, convenient doubt allowed Cement to omit the looming revenue from past diesel fuel rebates in the 2004 accounts or 2005 budgets. Budgeted profit before interest and tax for 2005 was a hundred and forty-five million dollars. When the diesel fuel rebates worth nine million dollars arrived early in the year, Cement was well on the way to a successful twelve months.

Cement calculated seventy percent of the monetary bonuses for those employees receiving bonuses by reference to the difference between actual and budgeted profit each year. In conjunction with low employee injury rates, most of us could suddenly look forward to a lot more money if we remained until the end of the year; my bonus could be thirty percent of my annual remuneration. People leaving voluntarily as late as December would receive no bonus at all. Putting aside my problems, I became what Keith, who worked at the Clyde depot and whose daughter was at school with my eldest daughter, called "another of the people just waiting to get their bonuses before getting out."

Money wasn't my only reason for remaining through 2005. I also wanted to complete my experience. More than being rude by turning her head away when I neared her, Sueki was being pathetic. It inspired me, if anyone was near her, to wish her a "good morning" or something as much. Compelling her to ignore me empowered me a little. When Colin was near us, I might even have laughed. He shouldn't know that I cared.

Company profit that year exceeded budgeted profit by ten million dollars, entirely attributable to fortunate windfalls likely but not certain when the budgets were prepared. Chris nevertheless lauded his success, nobly justifying it among executives in terms of employees "needing a win." Chris and the general managers stood to receive the largest bonuses of all.

Shareholders too could laud their successful investment; executive bonuses there also grew. Daisy chains can be long, even if the daisies dwindle in size.

In much the same way, an earlier Cement five-year plan forecast a profit of a hundred and sixty-seven million dollars in 2006. Directors were satisfied with the figure, so Chris saw no benefit in Greg's initial 2006 budget predicting higher profit. He instructed general managers (and particularly Greg) to reduce predicted revenues for the year (or do whatever else they needed to do) to reduce the budgeted profit back to the amount directors had already accepted.

Unfortunately, there'd been an error in the process developing the initial budget, as a Brisbane-based commercial manager told me later. When corrected, the forecast profit was back to a hundred and sixty-seven million dollars. I had no reason to remain.

My wife and I preferred to spend Saturday with our children than attend any Cement gathering. Several weeks before the 2005 Christmas party, I gave Sueki our apologies we weren't going. Neither she nor anyone else said anything to me at the time, but the signal of my dissatisfaction was practically tangible.

At lunch in the Greenwood Hotel, I told Martin I was looking for another job. I didn't know whether he'd mention it to Chris, but didn't care either way. I told a recruiter I was looking for a new role and was checking newspaper job advertisements.

Martin said I'd been wrong to talk openly about Sueki and the aggravation she'd caused me, although other people had also spoken of their experiences with her. Silence, and the isolation it brings, is professional etiquette.

Some tasks demanded my immediate attention, and I stayed back a little late New Year's Eve to document the agreed sale of the company's interest in a joint venture. Otherwise, my work through to the end of the year prioritised the two tasks that contributed to my annual bonus, including the pesky document register.

The human resources division had omitted to book the Couran Cove island resort when it published the dates for the third Cement leadership conference. So that year, the conference was convened at the Cypress Lakes golf resort in the Hunter Valley, New South Wales. I took photographs as a tourist passing through might've taken them, and mentioned to a few people that would be my last conference at the company.

A week later, Greg and I had scheduled my annual performance review. "Wayne will join us," Greg told me that afternoon, which sent my mind a wondering. The presence of anyone from the human resources division was normally a reason for dread.

Greg led us into Wayne's office, where Wayne closed the door behind us. My mind was racing. Performance reviews were always held behind closed doors, but Wayne closing a door was always reason to notice. Greg sat silently in a distant chair. I sat on one chair facing Wayne in another, across his coffee table by the clear glass wall. Wayne offered me six months' salary if I resigned.

I maintained my semblance of sombreness, while my silent mind roared, "Yes!" I imagined my fist clenched in ecstasy pulling through the air. "Whoa!"

Wayne said he'd decided to recommend to Chris that the company make me the offer that past November, but Greg had delayed it because I was busy with work. It could only have been the damned document register, along with that task I've forgotten.

Wayne explained the offer to leave by presuming I was searching for a new job but finding such a job would take time. He didn't want me leaving one year later when Chris was due to progress to his next company and Greg was due to return to the company from which he was officially seconded (or to the Australian American shareholder split from it shortly before Cement was formed).

In truth, I wasn't that important. Wayne went onto list other reasons leading him to make me the offer I wasn't meant to refuse, including downgrading my role (which he stressed by saying I would no longer attend executive dinners) and having upset the chief executive's personal assistant.

Wayne mentioned Chris being concerned about my reaction. When I assured Wayne I was relaxed about it, he keenly ducked into Chris' adjoining office to tell him.

The offer to me was supposedly conditional on Chris consulting with Jerry, the chairman. "In my experience," I told Wayne and Greg, "non-executive directors like to be consulted, but they don't intervene." (The independent director of Otter's listed subsidiary had complained that the chief executive hadn't consulted him about my appointment, although he was pleased about it having known of me from my first foray into local council politics when he supported an ally in another ward.) Wayne and Greg nodded.

Whatever Chris told Jerry, it probably wasn't the reason I was omitted from Jerry's farewell dinner, while the Swiss shareholder flew my predecessor Ron in from Brisbane to attend. It might, however, have been the reason that twice when I later applied for jobs at companies in which Jerry was concerned, I wasn't granted so much as an interview.

Nothing more was said to me until June, when concessions granted my successor made me question the sincerity of the role downgrading. Wayne couldn't remember anything of what he'd said to me back in February. To usher me out, he'd simply said whatever he needed to say. (Lies are more difficult to recall than facts.)

When I stipulated that my deed of release with the company refer to me having been made redundant, given the downgrading of my role, Wayne was adamant that the company wasn't going to be party to any taxation minimisation. (Some people are very altruistic with other people's interests.) He deferred the decision to the man he called "the big fella." Chris deferred to Greg, who had some expertise in the issue and lacked the imagination to lie. He agreed the company had downgraded my role sufficiently to constitute redundancy. (That was all in a business that expended a fortune in time and money on a dual corporate and partnership structure complicating its core, conducive to the taxation interests of a shareholder: the Australian subsidiary of an English company.)

Unlike most executives leaving, I worked through my period of notice, three months. I told Wayne and Greg that Shaun was my benchmark: I too would work hard. Whereas my address to the previous year's finance division conference was an introduction to law, Greg found something more important for me to talk about to my final conference. With my arms and hands motioning and my voice bold and resolute, I exuded every passion and sense of conviction any audience could see and hear in a speaker, talking of the new document register.

In truth, I did little work. Perhaps neither had Shaun. (If this was professionalism, then it was marketed professionalism.) I did even less after Sueki suddenly instructed my fifth and final secretary, the legal support officer Naomi, that I was to vacate my office that day, more than a month before I was due to leave. (Sueki had fired my fourth secretary Katrina, who like Dragana had a degree in marketing.) Nevertheless, I smiled and spoke positively of the rest of the company. I earned concessions (such as another month on the payroll and one more month's salary to be on retainer) I wouldn't have earned had I become embroiled with anyone's ego, but Sueki's.

A few employees asked me to let them know where next I worked, so they could try to come with me too. I don't think they were complimenting me so much as saying something about Cement. The payroll manager could hardly help but hark back to the days we both reported to Gary. "He was the best boss I ever had," Zoran told me. "He told you when you did something wrong, but he also looked after you."

In my last week at the company, in a conversation that hadn't required it, Wayne mentioned having a girlfriend who worked in human resources at another company. He might have thought my opinion of him might someday assist his career (if that wasn't me thinking too well of myself). I wasn't sure I believed him.

In that atmosphere, I asked him his age. He was forty-seven years old. He seemed much older.

In the last days of my retainer period, Sueki caught my final secretary laminating small posters for a church raffle at my request. She reported me to Wayne. Behind the glass wall and door of his office, she wasn't to know from his body language that he didn't care. Less than three years had passed since I began working there.

Possibly also to market himself to me, Wayne once insisted he tried to mitigate Chris' impact on the company: that Wayne was the soft touch. Throughout all my conflicts with Sueki and through my departure from the company, Chris never said anything directly with me. It was I that went to him at his desk my last morning and wished him well.

In my parting speech to head office staff, my last afternoon an employee, I mentioned a political novel I'd begun writing. I assured my audience that no character in the novel was modelled upon anyone there. I didn't mention this book, an idea in germination I'd not begun writing (although I'd been keeping a diary). Fictitious stories can make reality unreal.

Later in his office, Wayne was concerned to learn I was writing again. He might have feared what I might write or that I'd wanted the offer he'd made for me to go, that I'd engineered it. (In fact, I wasn't that clever. I was simply content for there to be no surprise when I secured another job and tendered my resignation.) Wayne went so far as suddenly to facilitate me getting a role with the major shareholder in Switzerland: a role I hadn't known existed. The human resources division never seemed to help employees entrusting their futures to it, but there was Wayne telling me he'd sent my résumé to Zurich. My knowledge of Swiss law was plainly inadequate, although he mightn't have known as much.

Sueki completely ignored the company's obligations to me in my deed of release through my retainer period, repeated in a memorandum to her before I left. Prematurely cancelling my company credit card and computer access hindered my work for the company during my retainer period more than it harmed me personally, but her motivations were never the company interest.

Still, I'd already received my redundancy money. Achieving what I'd wanted to achieve when I began working there, I repaid the last of my debts.

My deed also warranted that the six months' salary was at least as good as the redundancy package given any other executive, although Cement might have warranted something untrue. Unlike Shaun, my proportional bonus paid almost a year later was no more than my deed of release promised. (I should've told Chris that, by then, I was writing what eventually became this book.)

No employee really understood the reason he or she was dismissed although, the last time I saw her, a Tasmanian receptionist kindly remarked that the nice people went. Chris or Wayne mightn't have wanted me to choose my time to leave, when every departed general manager had been evicted.

Two years after my leaving, Chris and Greg were still at Cement. Only one explanation Wayne gave me for the offer he'd made for me to leave hadn't proven to be untrue: his allusion to me upsetting Sueki. Perhaps, not attending a second office Christmas party (which she'd overseen) was a career-*ending* move. Perhaps, it was the ballet school chocolates.

15

Truth and Lies

Along with governments pursuing subliminal votes, Australia's largest telecommunications company is among Australia's most prolific advertisers. A man attending a market research group with me mid July 2007 thought Telstra advertised itself with happy children, birds, clouds, and everything else because it wanted to be liked. He struggled to understand that Telstra wanted income. Simply being liked didn't matter.

Advertisements are often nice fantasies. They're fantasies nevertheless.

Two years after that market research group, I rather liked stumbling across a Telstra television advertisement set around a boardroom table in a tall city office building. A well-suited woman was addressing a meeting of similarly suited men and women when her mobile telephone, resting on the table beside her, sounded a tone. She glanced at the display. "Sorry," she told the people around her. "It's my Mum. I haven't called her in ages."

"How long has it been?" asked a bearded, much older man.

"Ah, three weeks," she guessed, "no, maybe four." Another woman shook her head disdainfully.

Staring at the first woman, the older man nodded his head. He pointed his eyes to her telephone.

"Thank you," said the first woman, picking up the telephone. "Hi, Mum. Listen I, I can't speak right now. I'm in the middle of a meeting…"

The advertisement was one of four in the 'Call Mum' series, I learned late that night from a website dedicated to the campaign. Even more fanciful and nicer would've been someone taking such a call from her son or daughter, but I suspect more mobile telephone users have mothers than children.

At the time, I'd never attended a board meeting at which anyone sat with her mobile telephone on the board table, although an American nominee director to the Cement board often sat reading messages from his Blackberry handheld device. Since then, Chinese directors and a West Australian director brought their mobile telephones to board meetings of Golden Cross Resources Limited, without interrupting meetings to take calls from their relatives. I don't believe the scene the Telstra advertisement portrayed occurs in any Western company.

In his strangely tiny, blue car, very new and polished, Wayne drove me into Sydney city the night a prominent Australian law firm invited its clients to the Dendy Cinema, Circular Quay to see *Enron: The Smartest Guys in the Room*. People unfamiliar with large Western corporations would've found the documentary a remarkable story of corporate greed, fraud, and atrocity; many a person trying to have fun could be destructive. Those of us working inside them were less surprised, although I don't think Wayne recognised anyone. He'd read the book, possibly looking for ideas.

The histories most likely to matter to Western businesspeople aren't family histories. They're company ones. (The company founder could've been a forebear, but still a family history means nothing.) In older industries, such as manufacturing cement, confidence among bankers and customers comes from carrying on business since 1892. In newer industries, confidence comes from trading since a week ago last Tuesday.

Records are better destroyed than retained. Maintaining them is a cost. Deleting them is easy. Laws normally require taxpayers and companies to keep only some records, and to keep them for just a few years.

Statutes of limitations encourage people and companies not already involved in litigation or pending litigation to discard records quickly. If a court order or government inquiry forces a person or company to produce its records, the last file in an old folder seems more often to harm than to help. The plaintiff wanting to sue or prosecutor wanting to convict normally carries the onus of proof in the West, so where evidence is insufficient to ground a conclusion, the defendant or suspect most likely escapes culpability.

Even among the innocent, trawling through records can be costly and cumbersome. It's not if records don't exist.

Three decades before the formation of Cement, the northern premerger company commissioned the writing of its history. Glorious pasts cajole people through changing futures, and Cement commissioned Judith, a past employee trained in history, to write its history, including the histories of the century-old premerger companies. Coaxing employees, customers, and suppliers through the merger required people like Jerry, Chris, and Wayne to talk of drawing on those two great traditions, until Cement's vision and values programme made history superfluous, at best. When history doesn't serve present objectives, we shed it.

At worst, history threatened the new company ethos. For anyone seeking real change, real history can really impede. While visiting the Brisbane office, Chris noticed Judith relaxing. He fired her.

Among the allocation of company responsibilities, human resources divisions normally create company histories. (Most things are the human resources division's responsibility.) The three panels of timelines and long series of old photographs across most of Cement's sites portrayed a hundred years of plants and furnaces, mines and minerals, without hinting at any context or culture. Production mattered, not people. Chris and Wayne chose the history they wanted.

Publicly, Chris and Wayne continued to talk of drawing upon two great traditions. Privately, they gloated over all they had changed. (Legal prohibitions on lying in trade and commerce don't prevent lies *within* companies.)

Every year, fewer people who'd worked for the two premerger companies remained. Few of them were so bold, except in small private conversations, to say how little remained of the places they once enjoyed working. Erasing real history requires erasing people who were there.

What some called the company's difficulty recruiting good people, Wayne called a careful and thorough selection process. While Wayne told us he'd made Cement an employer of choice, a recruiter (in conversation with the shipping manager) spoke of its reputation as a bad place to work. "Oh," said one recruiter to Kathryn, "I've heard about Cement..." She didn't need to explain why she'd left.

Wayne seemed to be on his way to a job with the Swiss shareholder managing its human resources in India, until suddenly he no longer was. Thus, he stood before my final finance division conference telling his audience that the shareholder's human resources department was incompetent and antiquated. (Calling it antiquated was probably a bigger insult than calling it incompetent.) Publicly lambasting Cement's largest shareholder surely breached at least two guiding principles, but no one bothered to mention it.

Somebody whispered that Wayne had wanted too much money. The Swiss shareholder already considered him overpaid.

Even more quietly, away from anyone's but my earshot, a

longstanding employee said the shareholder's employees didn't like Wayne abusing them when they didn't accede to him. Wayne would telephone the Swiss shareholder's head office and, if the person answering his call was someone he thought too junior for him, refused to speak with that person. The shareholder's employees found Wayne arrogant; amazing, really.

That final finance division conference was another venue at which Wayne boasted of the improved talent of people his human resources division recruited, which doubtlessly pleased those new people; there were a lot of them around. In truth, they were no more talented than the people they'd replaced, but few people left in the company knew.

The high turnover of staff at company sites in large towns and cities could have been a problem for Wayne, but his human resources division statistics buried it with the low turnover of staff at sites in small country towns with much less employment. Most attendees at my final finance division conference had been with the company no more than a year. In their well-prepared addresses, Wayne and Greg both said the many new faces reflected Cement being an attractive company to have on anyone's résumé. Other employers wanted to hire them.

Among the clever lies I'd heard, that one really impressed me. Greg couldn't have concocted it. New employees might have believed it.

Real history dispensed with, our postmodern West constructs new histories. What we don't choose, we create.

Among those drafting the new guiding principles soon after Cement formed, I'd been an executive but not a general manager. At my final leadership conference, the self-aggrandising film tribute to the new company referred only to general managers drafting them. (Colin hadn't been a general manager when he participated in drafting them either, but I guess we'd all forgotten that by then.) Writing me from history was certainly inadvertent (and the tribute did feature my work in trade practices), but the error didn't concern Wayne. What mattered was the ethos of unnamed general managers, not a lawyer soon leaving, settling the first draft of corporate commandments.

Values matter more than facts in our postmodern West, much more. So does retaining and motivating employees.

During his main address to the third leadership conference, Chris assured employees that Cement would continue to operate its old lime plant in Rockhampton. In reality, he was secretly trying to secure concessions from a competitor offering to manufacture lime at one of its plants, while simultaneously (and also secretly) trying to sell the plant to another company. Lying to employees is normally legal and ethical, retaining and motivating them when the truth would unsettle them, although I was struck by the fact that Chris didn't need to mention Rockhampton at all. This was no Machiavellian conviction that ends justify their means, but a complete indifference between fact and falsehood.

Chris' words were in my mind that evening, when I saw him walking from the accommodation villas to dinner. "I was thinking of you when I made my presentation," he said as we walked, "when I talked about Western Australia and South Australia."

I knew little of the company's plans in those two states, wholly unrelated (I presumed) to the plant in Rockhampton. Chris had revealed nothing illegal to the conference, but he left me wondering what he might be considering. He'd forgotten that executives and directors discussed those two states at a strategy day that past November, which I'd been due to attend until he or Wayne told Greg the preceding day I wasn't required. At the time, excluding me from that strategy day made me feel like a glorified minute-taker, until I realised I wasn't glorified at all.

I was barely remembered. Appearing in the third-quarter edition of *Vision* the year I departed was an article describing the tender process for the company's insurance broking: the last substantive work I performed at Cement. Crediting the tender with saving the company close to two million dollars a year suited us all, although the saving would have arisen without it.

Having done what I'd done with me no longer at the company made no sense, so instead of my smiling face heading the article, the consultant Bruce's smiling face did. What the audit committee had asked of me the article described as having been asked of Bruce, although the committee's only knowledge of Bruce had been my words in my reports to it (which committee members, other than Greg, might never have read). What I'd done, the article said Bruce did, without my trips escorting potential brokers and underwriters around plants. (Even if I'd drafted the article, I wouldn't have mentioned my trip to meet incumbent underwriters in Bangkok.)

Bruce never felt the need for a title, but he'd become treasury support manager. Old enough to retire, he and his wife would've liked children but were never so fortunate. She toiled away at her workplace, while Bruce worked to the extent Greg or I gave him tasks to complete and there was no game of golf in the offing or reunion among people with whom he and Greg worked long ago. When Wayne wanted permanent consultants made into employees for the company to control them much better, Bruce would've departed. He was cheap and good enough for Wayne not to press the point.

Bruce paid small regard for what the human resources division did. He would have drafted the *Vision* magazine article truthfully, before someone from the human resources division replaced my name with his throughout and gave him his title. No mere reader of the article would've known I existed, but for a single reference to Bruce doing what he did "*together with*" me, who'd been "*replaced.*"

The purpose of history so crafted isn't to record facts, but to serve management's present objectives. The magazine could have been called *Revision.*

Managers don't like employees too honest. They're terrified of what they might say.

Whenever company officers and managers are culpable for employees' illegal activities, they set up systems of corporate governance and monitoring not to prevent employees acting illegally, but to be their defence to being prosecuted when employees do. If they're making money from those activities, their individual interests make them prefer not to know those systems have failed. Chris avoided unwanted advice with an organisational structure by which the legal counsel and internal auditor reported to the chief financial officer rather than to him.

The second last Saturday in February 2009, Shaun was still at his role in a major recycling company when I saw him by chance in the Macquarie Centre. At the time, the Australian Competition and Consumer Commission was prosecuting Cement for arrangements the northern premerger company had established many years earlier, when Jerry was chief executive. Shaun believed, and said the commission believed, the man he called "that prick" had structured his role into a non-executive directorship to escape being personally prosecuted.

Retaining that sense of moral justice that made Shaun unsuited to our postmodern West, what irked him so much was the injustice of it all. I'd long stopped expecting anything else. My journalist friend Don, to whom I mentioned the gist of the story, and the journalist to whom he referred it didn't publish anything. Such behaviour wasn't news anymore.

By the time I ran into Shaun, Jerry was chief executive of the company that had owned half the *southern* premerger company. It was all just one day after another. Chief executives are an incestuous clique.

16

Childless Diversity

Model employees hope merely to endure, creeping up a few management tiers through the course of their careers. To rise any further when the only people in sight already concede everything to their work, we need one extra trait: the one vision and value that managers never demand from others. If they recognise it, they reserve it deep to themselves, wary of sensing it in somebody else for what it might mean to them. Unique to our post-racial, post-religious, individualist West, it's a willingness to condemn all life on earth to damnation, for the sake of one extra inch in the size of their offices.

The only female Cement Australia director (likely, I thought, to become head of the shareholder company employing her) encouraged consideration of women for all major roles. As my friend Ann-Maree, a business consultant and occasional lecturer at Macquarie Graduate School of Management observed, diversity at the most senior levels for most companies means diversity in gender.

Thus (or perhaps in any event), Wayne described as "fortuitous" the selection of a woman to succeed me as company secretary and legal counsel. A talented lawyer, Jackie might by chance have been the best candidate on merit, but she sensed the recruiter ushering her through. Interviewing Jackie for the role, the recruiter asked several commonplace questions. She then recorded answers that presumably made Jackie better suited to winning the job, but were different to those Jackie had given.

Cement promoted Jackie's appointment in the 'Diversity in Action' article in the following edition of its *Vision* magazine. Without other women among the executive team, the article commented that Jackie *"will form part of the Executive management,"* in spite of the role having been previously downgraded to be no longer executive.

Jackie was soon the first female face among the executive team on the company website, appearing at the end of what was otherwise an alphabetical male list. Her face remained there long after the end of her half a year working there, while quickly removed were the two male executives departing in that time.

The *Vision* magazine had long included mothers among the much-vaunted employee diversity. The 'Diversity in Action' article lauding Jackie's appointment didn't mention that the female recruiter had asked her, aged forty, "Do you have any children?"

"Asking me that question is illegal," replied Jackie.

"I know it is, but Cement…wants to get a picture of you." Jackie didn't answer.

At a later interview, Col asked her, "Do you have any children?"

That wasn't the time for a job applicant to be defiant. Jackie raised her fingers to show her wedding ring. "You can see that I'm married," she said.

Col, anointed to succeed Chris as chief executive, pressed her to state explicitly whether she had any children.

Finally, she relented. "No."

The communications manageress, a rare mother of two, had long expected my successor to be childless. Chloe was one of two employees to notice that few finance division employees had children.

One Friday, a few weeks after I left the company employ, my retainer required me to fly with Jackie to Brisbane. Far from the Cement head office, in the thick, black vinyl sofas of the Qantas Club lounge, Sydney airport, Jackie confided in me. "I don't know what's going to happen in a month," she said.

Her question had no basis in anything we'd been saying. We'd already told each other a lot.

"What do you think they'd do if I was pregnant?" Her question meant only one thing, but she hadn't confessed it to any current employee. "I know you like children," she explained, as her reason for entrusting me with the news.

Wayne, Col, and Chris were unaware that Jackie had been married for only a year. Soon after her interviews, she learned she was pregnant. "You're in now," I told her. "They won't do anything."

At about that time, July 2006, the Equal Opportunity for Women in the Workplace Association commended Cement for its reports of all it was doing to improve employment conditions for women. Naturally enough, the commendation featured in an article in the third-quarter edition of *Vision*, headed 'Women in business – leading the way in Cement…'

Jackie worked as late as she could before her baby was born. The company assured her she could return afterwards, working three days a week.

Among the applicants for the temporary contract role during her confinement, Karen (coincidentally, a lawyer with whom I'd dealt during my time at TNT) seemed poised to succeed. A few years more mature than Jackie, she too was clever, hard-working, and with an impressive résumé. Making her more certain she'd be awarded the role, Wayne sent her mail messages about Dunedin where both of them were born, in a brief hint of geographical kinship between them. Karen knew that what made her ideal was being female, unmarried, and childless.

Cement didn't offer her the job. Two years later, at a Christmas cocktail party convened by a legal recruitment firm in the Royal Exchange, she presumed it was because she'd said forcefully she would challenge anything she thought was wrong. Educated morons prevail over uneducated morons, but company-compliant morons prevail over independent-minded genii. No ideal candidate, woman or man, childless or a parent, is anything but compliant.

A man without obvious diversity was awarded the contract. All I know of him is that he posted comments to a news website supporting the Australian's government's deregulation of labour, which Chris, Wayne, and Col would've found particularly desirable. Perhaps no women but Karen had applied for the role. He never appeared on the company website, where Jackie remained.

When the time came for Jackie to return to Cement, Wayne told her the job was hers if she wanted it, but the role required somebody working full-time. We embrace women in our workplaces to work, disenfranchising them for profit from parenthood. In their pursuit of careers, some women oblige. Feminine traits concerned with nurturing, like those concerned with relationships, have been subsumed.

Jackie didn't oblige. She never returned to Cement.

After leaving Cement, I spent more time with my family and wrote; the company had given me so much to say. I searched sporadically for a job among the notices filling my computer screen to which I'd subscribed and among the advertisements in the Friday editions of the *Australian Financial Review* newspaper in our local and other public libraries. When recruiters to whom I'd sent my résumé called me, I responded.

The legal counsel at a drilling company liked that I was what the recruiter called "hungry" (a much nicer word than "desperate") for the well-paid and enticing associate general counsel role. More often than not, I felt passed over for roles for being too experienced (that was to say, too old). In that case, the recruiter told me the counsel preferred more experienced candidates. I was suddenly too young.

Later I learned that one of those candidates was an unemployed friend to whom I'd mentioned the role. In the confidences in which most people operate, even among friends, Duncan didn't mention he'd also applied. Twice divorced and childless, he was awarded the job. (It lasted only a year anyway.)

Duncan referred my name to another recruiter, who called me to fill a contract to work three months with insurance at the fund management business Babcock & Brown. The recruiter knew I was a parent, but if no one was hired, her recruitment agency received no commission. She wasn't going to admit anything to her client that might mean she'd receive no commission.

Through my two interviews with Carol at Babcock, neither of us mentioned children. I said nothing of my wife, so Carol had no reason to think I was anything but alone in the world. I would be late my first morning to attend a prior commitment, although the recruiter mightn't have passed along to Carol that it was a Father's Day breakfast at my children's primary school. She'd already awarded me the job.

I'm not sure why I felt the need my first morning at Babcock to mention my children. I did so in conversation with a softly spoken, unmarried analyst, with thick black hair and wearing enough make-up to keep her age indeterminate. Carol had asked her to show me the way to see someone on another office floor.

Later that year, Christmas Eve 2007, the Cement website declared Cement "*is very proud of its diverse workforce.*" It explained "*Why we embrace diversity,*" "*How we promote diversity,*" "*How our workforce reflects diversity,*" and "*Our partners in enhancing diversity.*" I checked the site because I'd received by ordinary mail the latest edition of the company's *Vision* magazine. Very few of the employees mentioned in the magazine I recalled from my time there.

There was diversity to be sure, a certain kind of diversity: childless diversity. Jackie's successor, the successor to the man in the contract role, was unmarried and childless. Less fortuitous than Jackie had been, he was male, but with an ethnically minor name and face. He quickly appeared on the company website.

Karen had worked with him at a previous employer, where his errors in one project cost a hundred and fifty million dollars. Cement's employment lawyer told our mutual friend David (who repeated his words to me over lunch the last Wednesday of January, 2008) that he had "no idea what he's talking about." Chris, Wayne, and Col would've found that an immensely desirable attribute.

When I saw him at a law firm lunch seminar the following year, I was struck by how short he was. Shortness might've been a problem for natural selection, but (in spite of Wayne's comments otherwise) could prove useful for its unnatural counterpart after all. Short men appear more likely to acquiesce and remain childless.

(Those appearances can be misleading. It appears he married and fathered children.)

"*Are you contemplating having children?' is the type of question a recruiter would ask to assess your future availability,*" advised a recruitment questionnaire I completed one Wednesday, almost a month after finishing my time at Babcock. "*In any case, answer no, even if you're planning on having a hoard of kids. This is actually what the recruiter wants to hear.*" Our careers are best served by being single and childless.

I presumed my non-fiction writing would end with the barest mention of Golden Cross Resources Limited, at which I worked after Babcock. I was wrong.

The chief executive Kim had worked at Otter before I worked there. We met through mining industry lunches, although I'd seen only his computer screen words and electronic mail address for nearly two years when he telephoned me at home one afternoon. The company's incumbent company secretary, legal counsel, and chief financial officer would soon leave. Instead of the professional services firms offering to perform the work, Kim wanted someone he knew in the tripartite role. I was also cheaper.

I began working there three days a week the thirteenth day of October 2008. Kim left me free to pursue other jobs, but I didn't. In my gratitude, I felt a personal obligation to perform well beyond mere professional duty and reputation (which was easy in a company without human resources personnel). The company's website biographies were of work, study, and for people without enough qualifications, memberships of professional associations. Spouses and children still mattered to me. Company biographies didn't.

The smaller the company, it seemed the smaller the people. This was the smallest company for which I'd worked.

The senior geologist's petty gripe was me ducking away from the office one workday for a haircut. He set it out in a series of electronic mail messages, copied to Kim.

The tenements manager (who claimed to work from home the days he didn't come to the office) tried to deflect Kim from blaming him for failing to renew a tenement by saying I worked too little. After Joe resigned, following a long holiday, the office manageress Carolyn and senior geologist absorbed his responsibilities.

Never were individual lives smaller than with the accountant, also employed there part-time. Carl stared at the floor in conversation; eye contact unsettled him. Defensively sitting with his back to his office door, he played solitaire card games on his computer.

The company employed Carl's daughter to clean the offices and, as time wore on, to fold notices to shareholders in envelopes. After I'd been at the company a couple of years, Carl decided I should complete time sheets describing my work each day. (The most stated reason for lawyers to leave law firms and join companies is to escape time sheets.) I didn't, so he withheld my salary.

Early in 2010, through a rare lunch at the Blue Gum Hotel, Kim again pilloried religion. "What is important?" I think I asked. "Sport?"

"No, I don't have a sporting team." Other people did. "You know the meaning of life better than most."

I could imagine only one answer.

"Children."

Kim was a devoted husband and father, but in our individualist West, devoted spouses and parents are only devoted to their spouses and children. During the meal, without the pretence that plagued other places, Kim told the young geologist Charlotte not to let relationships or families interfere with her work. The lives for which we want meaning are our own.

Many years earlier, Kim could've been killed in a hang-gliding accident, whereby his wife demanded he abandon the sport until their children finished school. (Many sports wantonly risk human life, but we think we're immortal or don't care. Our children compel us to care.) After his youngest son finished school, Kim perused websites for hang-gliders.

The only people at Golden Cross still procreating were the Chinese directors, Hui Xiao and Xun. Kim, Carolyn, and the company founder Dave cooed over Xun's baby.

After enthusing that the new Liberal Party leader Tony Abbott defeated the Australian government's plans for a carbon emissions trading scheme, Kim was furious when Abbott proposed a paid maternity leave scheme, funded by a levy on companies earning more than five million dollars taxable profit a year. (The company at which we worked was unlikely ever to be so profitable.) Interrupting his stride past my office, Kim bounced through the open door to tell me, "He'll lose business support."

Kim was right. Abbott never implemented the scheme.

Before the January 2010 board meeting, I showed Kim my draft response to a stock exchange proposal that companies report their efforts to increase diversity. Kim liked diversity when it meant more Chinese, but the stock exchange focused upon gender diversity. I'd drafted a policy supporting parents.

"I don't agree with any of this," said Kim as he read. (Never have I known anyone more honest.) "There's no allowance for parental responsibilities. There's no parental leave here." He hardly needed to say, "We're not family friendly. I don't want my employees having babies." He was quite explicit. "No one having babies should get in the way of work."

"Can I respectively suggest we don't put that in the report?"

We deferred the rest of our discussion until the stock exchange implemented the proposal. As it turned out, the Chinese shareholder nominated a female Chinese director, Jingmin, to replace Hui. We didn't need a gender diversity policy.

In 2013, workplace management consultancy Kronos published a survey of five hundred Australian employers, finding that forty percent preferred single employees without children. Only eighteen percent preferred those married with children. "The fact that a large majority of businesses thought that their ideal worker was a male, without relationships or interests and wants to work lots of hours, is particularly concerning," said Peter Harte, from Kronos.

Sex discrimination commissioner Elizabeth Broderick was concerned about employers preferring men to women. She seemed unconcerned about childlessness.

17

Fertility Ghettoes

My only colleague who stopped working when she married was a Lebanese accounts clerk at TNT Shipping & Development; we would have had a fit with a Western woman doing so. Rhonda was quiet and pleasant enough, with thick black hair contrasting against her skin uncommonly pale, but I don't think any of her colleagues heard from her again. She expected to mother as many children as she could.

When my grandparents were young, women often retired from their jobs when they married. My mother retired from hers when she first fell pregnant. We think we've changed so much since then, but if we changed to allow mothers in our workplaces, then we changed back again. Among the women at Holyman, only Jan was a mother. Theresa never returned after her baby was born.

We've made parenthood more difficult than it needs to be: labour without compensation or career. The children we bear not because of our circumstances, but in spite of them.

Before the merger forming Cement, a mother of four children single-handedly salvaged a cement plant not earning the profits the southern premerger company expected. Without ego or malice, Sandra dismissed employees that previous male managers had been unwilling to move. It seemed a little incongruous in a woman with long, greying, blonde hair spread so formidably from her shoulders, but Sandra never imagined that strength and resolve required her to surrender femininity. She helped me think women might generally be mentally stronger than men. More importantly, they might better understand we have group as well as individual interests.

After the merger, Wayne told Sandra that the southern premerger company had used her (as if companies didn't use people). Cement didn't use Sandra. It reduced her to entering data on its myriad of merger integration projects (like my document register), before dispatching her to manage a distant quarry.

The only parent of six children with whom I worked was Glen

Thomas. Like me, he'd worked at TNT, but after a long period of army service. He too had a Master of Business Administration degree, I think also from the Macquarie Graduate School of Management. For all our common history, we finally met when he became supply chain general manager at Cement. His commencement almost three months after mine was supposed to complete the new company executive.

Glen was seven years older than I was, with a healthy, full face and comfortable manner. When he broke his foot and was unable to drive a car, Shaun and I were among the people to collect him from his home of a morning and take him to work or take him home at the end of the day. Shaun would say, some years down the track, that he sometimes smelt alcohol on Glen's breath of a morning. I never did, although I wasn't checking for it. When Glen recovered enough to drive his car again, he bought Shaun and I each a bottle of wine.

Glen tried hard to be the sort of person Chris and Wayne wanted executives to be. While his underlings enthused to build a new ship, Glen imposed Chris' callous financial analysis. Glen wasn't "wedded" to anything, he told me dispassionately. "The easiest way to change the culture of an organisation is to change the people," he told me, amidst a conversation between us in the bright office kitchen. He learnt quickly to fire them.

It was never quite real. People reporting to Glen liked him. In his office were pictures of his family. He loved his second wife, Camilla, even more than he hated his first, but loved his three children from each marriage without favour. (He wasn't wedded to his first wife, either.) In private conversation, he called Wayne a "tyrant."

I knew Glen's job was secure. At an executive dinner, Glen mentioned that he might buy a boat. Chris suggested he talk about it to Col, who was also buying a boat. Chris wouldn't dismiss anyone buying a boat with Col.

Never did Wayne rush about head office with more passion and purpose than the day he wanted me to check the minutes of past executive meetings. Wayne was looking for mention that general managers were responsible for preventing employees within their divisions consulting directly with any of the three shareholders about working for them, ensuring they engaged Cement's human resources division and left everything to it. I found the mention. Wayne reviewed past employee circulars.

Catherine and Stuart had served notice they were leaving Cement to return to the major Swiss shareholder, without having involved Wayne's human resources division. Instead, they'd carried out their own conversations and correspondence with people they knew at the shareholder. Wayne tried to convince the Swiss shareholder not to proceed with their new jobs. He succeeded only in deferring Stuart's and, by a longer period, Catherine's departures, if that was some consolation.

By then, the general manager responsible for procurement was Glen. Chris and Wayne held him accountable for Stuart and Catherine escaping, like thieves in the night.

The following February was my third Cement leadership conference, where Catherine and I talked of her poetry and I told her of my sadness she was leaving so soon. (We didn't realise that I too would be leaving so soon.)

Late Thursday night, Glen was among several delegates drinking at the bar when Col summoned him to discuss fly ash distribution (as Col would, late at night at a conference). Glen didn't immediately come, which might've annoyed Col, as might Glen finally joining the meeting and blaming Col's sales and marketing team instead of his supply chain team for some problems with fly ash distribution. Whatever it was, Chris and Wayne dismissed Glen the following Wednesday. He would finish at Cement on Friday.

Wayne mentioned nothing about fly ash when he explained Glen's dismissal to me. (As was customary, I on the company's behalf reviewed the deed of release Glen would sign.) Instead, Wayne expressed sympathy for what he called Glen's alcohol problem.

I'd not seen Glen intoxicated, nor previously heard it mentioned. The business improvement manager I'd seen affected by alcohol at the conference, although Murray remained amicable and friendly while drunk. A rare Christian in that company, apparently, Murray kept that pretty well to himself. Murray was also another person Martin told me had problems with Sueki, but he also kept that to himself. Importantly, no employee reported to him, and so he couldn't have let any escape from the company to a shareholder. He never blamed Col for anything. Getting drunk at a management conference wasn't really a reason to fire someone (or there'd have been many more dismissals from many more companies).

Wayne went onto tell me that Glen had been cantankerous and bad-mouthing the company in the presence of a guest at the Thursday night conference dinner, stumbled drunk into the women's toilets, and nearly stumbled into a lake. Wayne claimed employees were crying out for redress against him, although I never found any even aware of what Glen had allegedly done. They were shocked Glen was leaving, as shocked as anyone still was at sudden departures from Cement.

With all the concern from his face of someone who cared, Wayne spoke to me of Glen's inability to cope with being an executive. He said Glen understood he had a problem with alcohol, and implied Glen was pleased for the chance to leave the company to deal with it. Wayne arranged for the company to pay for Glen to receive counselling.

Wayne made Glen the issue, not the company or its methods of management. Treating Glen as somehow mentally unwell maligned him more profoundly than simply dismissing him would've maligned him. (Glen might've had no desire to drink alcohol before coming to Cement, although that would be most unusual.)

The morning of the Friday he left, I sat with Glen in his office. I told him working with him had been a pleasure and that his departure was our loss. I wished him all the best. His termination payment would allow him to repay most of his mortgage debt. He said he planned to buy an investment property through a family trust or in his wife Camilla's name.

Later that day, I popped back to Glen's office to tell him Wayne had just offered me money to leave. We laughed. With a wave of his hand, he said that all those things I'd said to him that morning, he was saying back to me. We had no need to recall them.

Also dismissed that week was Christine M, renowned for working late in the office. The company was an equal opportunity firer, firing women and men with equal abandon.

A few months after Glen left, during the Ignite the Flame fair that local churches conducted on the St Ives Village Green each Anzac Day, I saw Glen by chance. Without much time to speak, we agreed to catch up again soon at the Greengate Hotel. Unlike most such agreements with people I'd known, we actually did. With my company credit card, I bought us each drinks, with alcohol.

Without being a community, we drive parents to exile. Childbearing and rearing are contracted away from swanky offices, shops, and homes to fertility ghettoes, where the rest of us don't hear of it. If those strongest and most intelligent people that companies don't hire were among them, then the whole process of unnatural selection mightn't matter so much, but they're in professions where their customers demand they be available and in universities with too much else on their minds.

Work is the priority. Ambitious employees rarely bear more than two children, one for each parent. Any more might intrude. They might bear just one, for the parents to share.

Demographer Nick Parr's report in the *Journal of Population Research* found that by 2001, university-educated women and those who didn't attend Roman Catholic schools were increasingly having just one child. They called them "higher quality" children and believed more parental attention would help those children succeed. It's a lonely sense of what constitutes success.

My stepmother called it "quality, not quantity." I assumed she meant the costs of private school fees and designer-label clothes for her only child, rather than anything about my children. She also said (I think to my wife) that motherhood wasn't glamorous (in spite, I suppose, of those fees and clothes).

Our natural desires wane a little more with each passing year. If we don't dispense with children altogether, we consign our unlikely offspring to others. If we haven't married someone to raise children we employ nannies to do so, while their husbands raise their children far away. Nannies are more compliant than fellow parents can be. They're also more readily dismissed.

Ideally for each of us so much the individual, we might think we don't need a fellow parent to share the costs and chores of parenthood. We might think we can parent alone. Scientists are now pursuing biological procreation without men and women: cloning offers replication without compromise.

We contract out rearing children and bearing them. Being keen to remain working, and to avoid pain, epidurals, and inconvenience, surrogacy motherhood is a womb for hire. The term of the lease is no more than nine months.

By 2008, more than fifty women in the Indian city of Ananda were pregnant with overseas Indian babies from America, Taiwan, Britain, and elsewhere, especially those couples with serious fertility issues. Paediatrician and ethicist John Lantos of the Centre for Practical Bioethics in Kansas City imagined the idea taking root with the West. (We believe everyone's the same anyway: those commodity wombs.) "You can picture the wealthy couples of the West deciding that pregnancy is just not worth the trouble anymore," he said, "and the whole industry will be farmed out."

What makes Western selection unnatural is that we're picking others, not us, to procreate. The people we won't risk losing are the people we rarely see; parenthood persists among people we want tending to stores, cleaning offices, and collecting garbage. Unnatural selection propagates people natural selection might abandon.

With or without income and other means tests, government assistance to parents risks making parenthood a job like any other, albeit for many a temporary assignment. Subsidies favouring single parents discourage them from marrying. For people to bear children for money, the income to procreate must be their best income available.

Most of us forgive too much income (not to mention our careers) through periods of confinement for mere subsidies to entice, except at the margins of decision. We take the money for raising children we would've raised anyway. Unlike other Australians collecting their baby bonuses, apparently, my wife and I didn't buy a plasma television set.

The values that matter to us are those related to commerce. The West expects education for vocation (along with mass marketing) to dictate the values of commodity children. The weakest and stupidest of people can still become employees and consumers. We might even prefer them like that.

One evening during my time stationed in a Washington law firm, and many other evenings besides, the firm brought poor children into its meeting room, away from the offices in which people were working. The firm wanted to show those children they too could be lawyers. (It did mean to be kind.)

Babcock & Brown employees mentored other people's children: year-nine students at the Bass Hill and Hoxton Park High Schools. Each mentor encouraged a young person "*to achieve a productive working and personal life.*" That was to say, to become like a mentor.

By our work and wealth, we're trying to procreate our values and character, but not our families and race. The male mentors from Babcock would've been distinguishable from drug dealers by their cufflinks.

Come October, almost two and a half years since I'd left Cement and about the same time since I'd last seen Glen Thomas, his two youngest daughters were girl guides in blue dresses in the troop of which my wife was a leader. Camilla was among the mothers assisting her through a weekend at the Glengarry camp. Camilla and Glen were divorced, although Camilla said their marriage had been ideal for the first seven years, until about the time Glen left Cement.

Camilla spoke of what a dysfunctional workplace Cement had been, but Glen's intermittent working life since then seemed to have brought their marriage down. When my wife mentioned my working life had also been intermittent since Cement, Camilla said of me, "At least he's kept his family together."

Somewhere in Hornsby, where I was working at Golden Cross Resources Limited, Glen was an alcoholic, living alone in a home unit. I thought of calling him, but didn't know what to say. Camilla thought he could only live there for about six more months, before he'd be homeless. She'd know that time had come when she deposited a cheque he'd sent to maintain her, but the bank dishonoured it.

18

The Success of Solitary People

I asked a particularly pointless director standing with me in my Holyman workstation whether he had children. "No," replied Ted.

Silently in my mind, I thought to myself, "On behalf of the human gene pool, thank you!"

That was my stupidity. The rift between directors and others in our little, mortal company distracted me from bigger issues.

Only four of my dozen or so colleagues at the Otter head office had children. Phil had two. Pat, Ros, and Krystyna had one each.

Among the five people in Sydney reporting to Carol at Babcock & Brown, only I had children. Devoted to her husband, Carol had stepchildren and step-grandchildren. She, Gavin, the softly spoken analyst, and even the generally amicable Angela complained of the behaviour of children in shopping centres. Even more than the children, they complained of the parents.

Kevin was the only other parent among the dozen or so people reporting to Enzo, having become so just before I arrived. (Apparently a polyglot of races, the human resources division would have loved Kevin.) Enzo had two children, I think. When a baby (Kevin's I think) was brought into the offices, well away from their desks, Gavin and our secretary complained that babies shouldn't be there. Gavin went onto complain that the same thing had happened at the offices of an insurance brokerage firm for which he'd previously worked. That baby drove him and other employees to the furthest corner they could go.

Knowing which employees at the Cement head office were parents was difficult. Glen Thomas had six children, but he was dismissed. Shaun and John each had three, but they too were dismissed. Most had one child or were childless, before Joanna bore twins.

Kitty, Peter's personal assistant in Melbourne, told me two days before Christmas 2004 that she would spend Christmas alone before a friend visited her that evening. With no family since her grandmother died, Kitty lived with her cat.

To build a head office team, oblivious to everything we'd seen, Wayne convened a sailing day on Sydney Harbour one weekday afternoon. Without real senses of being groups, the teams that companies vaunt are tools by which nominated team leaders and everyone else exercise their individual interests. (Perhaps Wayne just wanted to sail.)

Before Cement formed, Colin worked for the southern premerger company, assisting Greg. He was a large man with a crooked, clumsy limp, as if a long-suffered injury to his hips as much as his weight affected him walking. His accent was apparently not South African, but Zimbabwean. Referring to their cricket team in my first months at the company, Chris flippantly described white Zimbabweans as "displaced farmers."

The first full-year budget for Cement included provision for more payments to redundant employees. When a draft was presented to executives, the normally congenial Colin asked anxiously, "What are the redundancies?" Perhaps he asked, "Who?"

Chris named the people concerned. Colin wasn't among them.

"Phew," sighed Colin.

Executives laughed. Chris smiled.

Colin was initially the integration manager, responsible for establishing the new company head office. He then became responsible for nagging the people responsible for implementing the scores of initiatives the merger supposedly allowed. He soon became a general manager with one assistant and then a second (Sandra) to help him nag. (After giving instructions and information, most managerial communication becomes nagging.)

In a conversation late one Friday night, aboard an aircraft coming home, I asked Colin all manner of things unrelated to work (although nothing about his limp). Like Greg, Colin was an atheist. (As for that matter surely was Chris, Wayne, Sueki, and Col, if ever they thought about it.)

When Colin complained that the northern premerger company had been "unprofessional," he meant that its employees didn't work long enough hours. (We regard anyone expending five hours to complete a task as inherently more dedicated than someone completing the task in only two hours.) Colin's six-day working week encompassed being in the office each Saturday, while his wife worked elsewhere. Their children no longer lived with them. (I'm not sure which caused which.)

In addition to his designated responsibilities, Colin reviewed the work of his fellow executive, the manufacturing general manager John.

Colin described John to me as "dishonest." Chris removed strategy and projects from John's responsibilities and gave them to Colin. Colin continued reviewing the rest of John's work until John was dismissed, but instead of adding manufacturing to Colin's portfolio, Chris and Wayne recruited a new manufacturing general manager from the Swiss shareholder.

Colin thereafter reviewed the work of another fellow executive, the supply chain general manager Glen. Colin derided Glen to me as a "show pony." Glen too was dismissed, but instead of Chris appointing a replacement, Colin subsumed supply chain responsibilities. Finally, Colin had his own work to occupy six days a week. No other employee's title changed as frequently as did Colin's: the general manager for whatever he could get. In an atmosphere of recurring dismissals, that might've been his strategy to survive.

Distracted by one trivial event, Colin drolly remarked that it would soon be the subject of a company video. His dry wit was a brave mocking of Wayne, although only I was there to hear him. He might've trusted my discretion.

Privately to me, Colin disagreed with the way Chris treated people, when I was one of those people. Publicly, I never saw him disagree with Chris. Glen pointed out to me that Colin sat beside Chris at executive committee meetings, whenever he could.

I suspect politics made Colin eat lunch with Sueki instead of coming to my farewell lunch. Throughout the conflict between her and me, Colin was far more concerned with her Asian desire to keep face than with anyone else's sensitivities. (White people aren't so interested in keeping face ourselves.) With them was the gently mannered receptionist Gisella, careful not to upset her mistress.

Unobtrusively, Colin had risen to form part of Chris' secret inner cabinet: Chris, Wayne, Col, and Colin. For all their apparent differences, the ruling central clique shared an extraordinary consistency of values, completely estranged from the values they publicly pronounced. Chris insisted executives act like a team, but even Martin often insisted he didn't "know what's going on." Most notably, at least to me, Martin said he "hadn't seen that coming" when the company offered me money to leave.

Greg, to whom I reported, seemed equally uncomfortable with me leaving. He'd disagreed with the offer being made to me, but not enough to change anything. I expect he couldn't. He wouldn't have been appointed to his role if he were the sort of person to try.

Bob labelled the clique, "the in crowd." He particularly lamented my departure because, like the rest of the departing and him, I was not. A rare executive to reveal personal details in his biography on the company website, Bob was married with two children. The biography didn't mention that he and his quietly spoken wife adopted a child, before unexpectedly conceiving their own.

With Bachelor of Engineering and Master of Business Administration degrees, Bob was probably the most academically qualified of all general managers. As tall as Wayne and a handful of years older, Bob was lanky, with hair a pale shade of grey and face long and thin. Most importantly, from Wayne's point of view, he was general manager for safety, health, environment, and quality. Those responsibilities were probably listed in that order so they more readily became an acronym. Bob was the SHEQ G.M.

He'd joined Cement a few months before Wayne and I did. Walking together around the streets of Gladstone early one spring evening, shortly after I started working there, Bob, Greg, and I leisurely climbed a park to a small lookout. From there, we gazed above the trees and grasses to the open blue sound and sprawling blue ocean. Bob mentioned having worked for thirteen years at his previous company (the same company from which Greg was still officially seconded) and thirteen years at another before that. He came to Cement expecting to spend thirteen years there before retiring. It all seemed very neat.

Soon after starting at Cement, Wayne tried to demonstrate his understanding of occupational health and safety by asking his audience of employees to identify the worst safety hazard around them. They dutifully looked about. Some might've guessed electric ceiling lights, others high windows. If the steel-framed chairs with moulded plastic for sitting collapsed, they could hurt people. Employees guessing any of those risks would have been wrong. The tall Wayne slowly reached his arm up to the ceiling, until his fingers were close to a tiny crack or hole. From it, he removed a little metal paper clip.

The supply chain development manager telling me the story went on to say that, for a while, some employees called Wayne "P.C." for his effort. The name didn't last.

Bob was no less passionate about safety than Wayne, but much less passionate about paper clips. At the first leadership conference, he gently chided me for climbing stairs two stairs at a time. "As an executive," he told me, "you should be setting the example."

Moving up and down stairs safely was a specific theme of that conference, with a guest speaker delivering an address about it. We should proceed one stair at a time with one hand holding the handrail or bannister, and without speaking to anyone. Throughout the ensuing days and nights of the conference, Cement employees didn't just use stairs as we'd been told to use them. We scrutinised other employees as they used them.

(It worked. To this day, I walk up and down stairs as I learnt to walk them during that conference, apart from the silence. I insist my children do the same.)

Wayne increasingly involved himself in matters within Bob's portfolio. His criticisms of any safety problem or environmental incident among the company businesses were the fiercest of his fierce criticisms in executive meetings. When he pulled back from a personal attack on Bob, everyone else in the room was supposed to think that only some sense of courtesy, even professional decorum, restrained him.

Also increasingly, Bob wore his fluorescent yellow safety shirts not just at plants but at offices. Perhaps they were protection from Wayne, or perhaps Wayne wanted him to wear them so Wayne saw him coming.

The man who once spoke freely became private. Several months after she became his secretary (as well as Martin's and my secretary), Bob had spoken so little with Joanna of matters aside from their work and paid so little attention to her hands, he was unaware she was married.

Bob's privacy didn't deter me from telling him of my problems with Sueki banishing me to a corner office. He said the half a dozen or so personnel reporting to him called it being "Wayned."

Bob dealt with those personnel reporting to him in much the same way as he responded to me scaling the stairs: pedantically, but politely. (I consider pedantry a virtue.) Those personnel seemed to like Bob and respect him, but the only one with whom I spoke freely, over lunch in Melbourne the week after my final leadership conference, knew Wayne didn't like Bob. When we speculated who might be the executive that Wayne told me the previous day was about to be fired, Henry guessed it was Bob. In fact, it was Glen.

I didn't tell Bob (or anyone else at Cement) that in the conversation in which Wayne offered me money to leave, he also said Bob would shortly become a consultant. Less than three years had passed of the thirteen that Bob initially planned to spend at Cement, but so much had changed since we looked out from that grassed hill in Gladstone.

Before I finished my time at Cement, Wayne told me, "Bob and Chris have sorted out their differences." That meant Bob had persuaded

Chris to let him remain, better than Wayne had persuaded Chris to remove him.

No amount of compliance was going to let Bob remain there forever, or even for that thirteen-year plan. He needed to fight as relentlessly and ruthlessly to keep his job as Wayne fought to take it from him; guiding principles didn't enter into it. To survive, Bob needed to become like Wayne: tirelessly manipulating Chris into firing Wayne before he was fired.

Bob didn't. Within a year, he departed. Wayne finally succeeded in subsuming safety, health, environment, and quality within his little doll empire, while Bob returned to his family. Wayne, with his empty home and photographs in his office, became the general manager people and performance.

Sueki finally left Cement. When Wayne by chance saw the former secretary Jill, he joked about Sueki, "She might have some real work to do now!"

Sueki, Wayne, and Chris had seemed a tight, unified unit, sitting in adjacent offices and her adjacent workstation. I doubt any of them ever liked any other.

Attending our parish Anglican church was a semi-retired engineer (and non-executive public company director), with whom I spoke most when I saw him by chance at the Greengate Hotel, one Friday evening of 2008. Reflecting upon the changes he'd seen through his working life, Bill complained that businesspeople no longer confronted people and issues. Instead, we'd become sneaky.

Personal conflict can be relationship, but the West no longer does relationship. We just leave the room.

Later that year, no doubt alone, Wayne moved to Zurich. He wasn't seeking refuge, but rising to a new role with Cement's Swiss shareholder company; Swiss people ought to have been seeking refuge. Wayne became the behemoth's vice president for global talent acquisition.

All his title meant was human resources, whatever that meant. The title alone ensured that employees the Swiss company hired were talented. Otherwise, Wayne and his division wouldn't have hired them. Language dictates perception, titles become self-fulfilling. Wayne would surely prove his worth by saying people hired by the company before he arrived weren't so talented. He would set his sights upon some of them in another list turning over, for no other reason than he could. Somewhere on a shelf in his office, would probably stand his photograph of another man's wife.

In our unnatural West, survival of the fittest means individuals seeing themselves solely as individuals, without families or races. Other individuals don't deter them from their pursuit of whatever they want.

Solitary people foist solitude upon others. To survive and succeed, we'd become what Chris long wanted employees to be, quite apart from whether we work on our cars. We became self-reliant not simply because we wanted to be, but because we needed to be.

19

Stress

Working hard isn't stressful. Stress is something else altogether.

The distinction between real health and health in our postmodern West is starkest in cases of stress. For company chairmen like Jerry, executive stress is choosing what luxury motor car to buy. With every next layer of management downwards and diminishing control over our lives, stress becomes more acute. Stress causes a person's body to produce cortisol, which increases weight and damages nerve cells including brain neurons, particularly as a person ages. We become fat and stupid.

Addressing my final finance division conference, in a huge room at the Brisbane Riverview Hotel, Chris justified Cement's propensity for firing employees by his desire to improve his standard of living each year (although his standard of living was already pretty good). He expected attendees to want improved standards of living, too. He expected us to be like him.

Financial security, families, and communities were all excluded from Chris' concept of standard of living, at least as regards other people. Not only didn't Chris care about employees fretting over how they'd meet their next mortgage debt repayments, working long hours to keep jobs they didn't like, and being fired, neither should anyone else. We needed to fret only about our own financial predicaments, disappearing time on earth, and social isolation. (That's individualism.)

With so much of the company product sold to two of its three shareholders, Chris could do little about revenue to improve company profits. (Chris and Col wouldn't make Shaun's blunder of doing anything at those shareholders' expense.) Chris thus told an executive committee meeting that he wanted "people to lie awake at night, thinking about costs."

By costs, he meant company costs, rather than their personal and family's costs. In fact, they were more likely to lie awake at night thinking about losing their jobs; nothing unsettles employees more than seeing their colleagues fired for something other than faults. (Faults they can often remedy or avoid.) "Are you scared of losing your job?" Wayne asked one employee.

"Yes."

"Good."

Most stress that managers inflict is more reckless than deliberate or malicious. Fearing the company's liability to compensate employees for harming their health, Wayne insisted no manager talk of stress and no company records refer to it. I tried to satisfy him we could refer to "alleged stress" each time an employee claimed stress, and the human resources division investigated and rejected the claim.

Through those Cement years, for the first time in a decade or more, I again came across Sarah. She'd been assistant company secretary at TNT while I was company secretary for TNT Shipping & Development. With her, four floors above my office, she reported to a man with a shining black moustache beneath his shining black hair. Walking with a slight stoop in his shoulders didn't keep him from being appointed TNT company secretary. It might even have helped. (Company secretaries are like that, say I having been company secretary.)

A two-tonne elephant barging towards him wouldn't have stirred the unflappable moustached man. The group legal counsel complained that he made much of arriving at his office at eight o'clock in the morning, but then read a newspaper for an hour before commencing work sometime thereafter. (I didn't arrive in my office until nine o'clock, often slipping into a side door because I was late. I read newspapers later.)

After I'd become company secretary for TNT Shipping & Development, the moustached man returned minutes of meetings and other internal company documents not complying with the TNT company manual. I might've written dates with months before days or days before months, or days with or without ordinal suffixes (such as "2nd" instead of "2" or "2" instead of "2nd"), or whatever, whatever, whatever. I expended more time rewriting them as he wanted. The directors who'd signed them expended more time signing them again.

The moustached man sent me one memorandum copied to an audience commanding me to do something he thought was important. I replied with a memorandum copied to the same audience, assuring him that I did. He then telephoned me to abuse me for wasting everyone's time by sending such a memorandum.

During one TNT crisis, the United Kingdom finance director sent him a letter by facsimile transmission. His only reply was refusing to read the letter, because it was not in the official company font. With a day lost, Clive sent the letter again, with the correct font.

(Clive told me this story when he later joined Holyman. With public documents I was very particular, but I assured Clive that internal company documents needed only to be easy to read.)

Neither Clive nor I reported to the moustached man. Sarah did. A lawyer, Sarah groomed her fair hair high and close to her head, while powders covered her fine facial features. Her firm English accent easily became high-pitched when her work made her passionate. Her responsibilities included using a ruler to measure the relative size of the letters and boxes in which they stood in the company logo on company documents, ensuring they complied with the company manual.

Once, entering her office, I saw she'd been crying. Quickly, she wiped her eyes dry. Corporate etiquette (I'd not yet learned to breach) required me not to comment.

More than a decade later, TNT had shrunk to be a subsidiary of an overseas post office. The former TNT Tower One had a new name and tenants. Gathering dust in old boxes were old company minutes and documents in the correct company font and with dates written in the company style, if they'd not long been destroyed. If anything remained with the old company logo, then every letter and box were in their proper proportions.

After a brief time with another ill-fated company, the moustached man was again TNT company secretary, but of a much-reduced entity. When next I saw him, some years later, his moustache and hair had turned grey. If he wasn't weary with age, then he'd learned to relax. Conversation between us came more easily than it had, even when I'd asked him about his newborn son all those years ago. I like to think he'd learnt that those things that once seemed important weren't really important. I know I had.

Sarah and I had long left TNT. Ending her ten-year hiatus from a legal career to raise her daughter, Sarah sat a job interview at eight o'clock one Monday morning. Only at the interview did the young female recruiter, from one of Australia's best known legal recruitment firms, read the résumé that Sarah had sent her the previous Friday. She told Sarah, "You haven't done anything for ten years."

"I've been raising my daughter."

"Do you know want I'm going to do?" replied the recruiter. "I'm going to end the interview now."

Before she departed, Sarah told the young woman that when she was a mother, she'd understand the importance of raising her children. Sarah hoped she'd then remember what she'd said that morning.

The young woman was silent.

"Goodbye," said Sarah.

Sarah was the sort of intelligent and conscientious person who, were our species still enjoying natural selection and workplaces wanted productive labour, would have risen further in her career, if she'd wanted to do so. Instead, she was never again a company employee. She would also have born several intelligent, healthy, and beautiful children, but she bore only one. She would've liked to have more children than the daughter (a champion rower) she was lucky to bear, but felt the stress of reporting to the moustached man at TNT meant she struggled to fall pregnant.

Our corporations have become contraceptives, to which we concede not just our lives but our futures. Without our senses of race and religion to save us, free market economics empowers the people who'd end Western childbearing.

The moustached man wasn't the only source of stress in Sarah's job at TNT. When Sarah asked a junior solicitor at a major Australian law firm to perform a task and to do so urgently, a partner from the firm telephoned her. In spite of TNT being so important a client, Peter Cameron abused her. "You're to give instructions to *me!*" he yelled.

Peter also led the team that helped us establish Holyman. A decade or so older than I was, then in his early forties years of age, he was tall with hair so thin it made his face seem particularly oval, although it was really no more oval than most faces were.

He might've been one of only two people I've known through my life to use the word "otiose." The other was my mother, although she'd merely spoken it, most likely quoting her father. I thus took a moment to recognise it in a letter addressed to TNT Shipping & Development (I can't recall if Peter was the signatory), which drew great attention from Reuben, the finance director. The word seemed not only archaic and erudite, but pompously so. The letter taught me how to spell it.

Around about the New Year becoming 1994, Peter sent us by facsimile transmission a short letter informing us the new company Holyman had been incorporated. Optimistically he added, in the brief levity New Year could bring, "*A star is born!*"

Not simply for using words like "otiose," Peter was among the people least likely to abbreviate his (or anybody else's) name. Hearing Stuart (with whom I'd studied at law school almost a decade earlier and I came across by chance at a seminar or cocktail function) refer to Peter so irreverently (although affectionately) as Camo was quite incongruous. The nickname reflected more of Stuart's personality, than it said anything of Camo.

Another decade later, long after the Holyman star collapsed into a black hole, I sometimes saw Camo striding along city footpaths. Still tall in his dark suits and with his hair becoming still thinner, I would've presumed he was walking between appointments even without papers in his hands. I never imagined Camo anywhere except between appointments, or dinners like the one he hosted for us after setting Holyman on our way. If ever I smiled at him so many years onward, we never paused to talk.

Camo achieved everything in his career that, long ago, we young students dared want. Law school lecturers of mine had become High Court judges, but the ivory towers most of us dreamed of climbing were law firms like Camo's, probably the most celebrated of Australian firms.

Because I'd known him, Peter Cameron's name stood out among the names of directors in an infamous building products company (his name wasn't reported as Camo). Before moving its registered office far from Australia, James Hardie had set aside too little money for a trust fund to compensate past employees and customers dying because they'd been exposed to asbestos.

While directors were fielding no end of criticism from trade unions, governments, and victims, I'm not sure I noticed Peter Cameron's retirement from that company board for ill health. A journalist writing for the *Crikey* website scoffed at him sneaking away, as surely many people did. Six weeks later, in the month Wayne offered me money to leave Cement, I read the journalist's apology. Peter had died from cancer at an age around about my mother's age when she too died young, fifty-five years old.

I sent a message to my former Holyman colleagues telling them the sad news. The former Holyman finance manager (another Peter) thought I was joking to call the news sad; he would have welcomed any public company director's death, lawyer or not (and possibly any lawyer's death). Reuben realised the blemish to Peter Cameron's name brought by that asbestos controversy was merely a blemish.

That law firm of which he'd been a partner marked his passing with a memorial notice in a newspaper, referring to his widow and children. If, during the months we set up Holyman, Peter mentioned his family, I wasn't listening. He didn't need to mention his family to us for it to matter to him.

Importantly for me, his death made insignificant the great success Peter achieved in the law. Similarly insignificant was the law firm career that youthful I aspired to make and older I sometimes missed. Peter Cameron's wisdom and wit seemed suddenly so memorable and to matter so little, aside him being a man, husband, and father.

Three years after his death, Sarah told me the story of Peter abusing her. That stress convulsing him seemed, at least to Sarah, a reason he might've developed cancer. If she was right, then the means of his success might've killed him.

To Stuart and Tim at our twenty-fifth anniversary dinner after our Supreme Court admission, Camo contracted cancer because of the stress brought upon by the asbestos controversy. They said the asbestos controversy also drove another partner of Peter Cameron's law firm (a past recipient of a university medal no less) into a mental breakdown, with his colleagues finding him standing atop the building in which he worked, and eventually into leaving his wife and daughters. A homosexual man caught up in the controversy committed suicide. I didn't know enough to disagree.

Camo wasn't the first lawyer I knew to die from cancer. Maria Tirabosco and I had been students together, applying for summer clerkships before our last years of law school. The first time I attended law school not in my jeans and other casual clothes was the day I left early to attend my first interview at a law firm, wearing my only business suit and trousers. The appointment immediately adjacent to mine was Maria's; she wore a sharp brown suit and skirt. Nervously, I sat beside her in the Cutler, Hughes, and Harris reception area. I didn't get the job. She might've.

I don't think I saw much of Maria during our working lives, until I replied to her advertisement soon after I left Holyman. Maria had founded Sydney Outsource Legal Services placing lawyers on contract so she could work from home with her young child. Two years later and without me seeing her again, seventeen years after I'd sat so young and anxiously beside her in that law firm reception area, she died. A small part of my personal history as I was a small part of hers, she was just thirty-nine years old.

Her legal contracting business endured because her widower husband wanted it to: another legacy of her. Five years onward, at the end of my time with Cement, I spoke with a recruiter from Sydney Outsource Legal Services. She did not know who Maria was.

All our careers had become unimportant. Their only consequences are the children they'd kept Sarah from bearing.

Much had changed since Sarah started her legal career when, in spite of the stresses, she could ask older, more experienced people (like the moustached man) for advice. Companies no longer carried middle levels of manager with time and mind to advise, she said in a long conversation in my office at Golden Cross Resources Limited.

Helping people is no longer the norm for people with advice to proffer. It's a task reserved for a plethora of dedicated professionals charging fees for their guidance, such as Martin spoke of becoming at Cement. To the extent we aren't already self-reliant, we can learn to be self-reliant from the company's nominated mentors or from career coaches we pay, maintaining our spaces apart.

Sarah no longer worked in what her mentor called "the dog-eat-dog world" that corporations had become. That was Western individualism.

As well as some consultancy company secretarial work, Sarah was using her knowledge and career experience to teach the English language to immigrant businesspeople and their children. I'd referred to her my colleague (in a manner of speaking), the business development director (of sorts), Hui Xiao.

Hui must've been pleased with her tutoring. Soon, she was also teaching English to what Hui called his personal assistant. Wenjun's role, initially that of a photographer, had become more like one of a driver.

20

Sustainability

In 1995, the lecturer in the cross-cultural management course of my Business studies distinguished Europeans and Latin Americans that worked to live, from North Americans that lived to work. Since then, North Americans have prevailed through much of the West. If we don't live to work, we live to spend.

Consumers rarely look past the point of consumption, for that would be like watching our weight instead of savouring a cream puff. (We like to do both.) When consumers look past the moment, it's normally no further than the date of our next credit card statements. As a lecturer during my studies for my economics degree expressed it, "In the long run, we're all dead."

Commercial interests making childlessness compulsory were never more explicit than in the case of Canadian singer Nicole Appleton. In 1998, with her band All Saints at the peak of its success, Appleton was eagerly looking forward to her baby conceived with her fiancé, British singer Robbie Williams. He'd told her the baby would save his life, giving him reason to fight his addictions to alcohol and drugs. He went so far as to decorate a nursery for the child, for whom he chose the name Grace should she be a girl.

The band's name, All Saints, was mere marketing: a fraud. London Records and bandmate Shaznay Lewis pressured Appleton to abort her child. The record company convinced Appleton's sister Natalie that abortion was in their band's best interest. "*I was horrified,*" Appleton wrote later in her book *Together*, "*violated by what I felt was the power of an industry that leads a woman to sacrifice her child to keep a band together. What mattered was our success and our ability to make money.*"

Four months into her pregnancy, Appleton surrendered to her record company's demands. She remained awake through the procedure, seeing her child on the scanning equipment. "*I wanted to shout 'No, No!'*" she wrote, "*but it seemed impossible. Suddenly, horribly, I*

145

realised, with a clarity that rocked my entire body, what had happened. My baby had gone. I fainted."

The abortion nearly pushed her to suicide. She and Williams ended their relationship soon afterwards. All Saints' success didn't last.

Women in the West have no right to a child, but have quite a right to abort. Powerful people have the right to mould their exercise of their right.

Until 2011, the Royal College of Obstetricians and Gynaecologists advised pregnant women that rates of psychiatric illness and self-harm were higher in women who'd had abortions. Draft new guidelines that year reversed that advice. They suggested doctors, nurses, and counsellors tell pregnant women abortions were safer than carrying a baby. (However safe we've made childbirth, even the slightest risk of incident is greater than none.) *"Although abortion can be associated with a range of feelings,"* said the guidance, *"long-term feelings of guilt, sadness and regret appear only to linger in a minority of women."*

"The message this sends out is very worrying," objected consultant psychiatrist Patricia Casey, a fellow of the Royal College of Psychiatrists. "There are more than thirty studies showing an association between psychological trauma and abortion."

Like so much else about our postmodern West, the new guidelines could be traced back to money. No psychiatrists were among the people drafting them. Contributing to them instead were two of Britain's largest abortion clinics.

At best, many a manager focuses upon the next accounting date by which his performance is judged and her bonus determined. (Capital investments can stretch their horizons along useful lives of assets, for which accounting treatments make allowances.) Chief executives often fleet into companies, accruing quick, good results by stripping out employees and other costs. They leave before the disasters they've created are realised.

Colin complained to me that Chris' motivation for agreeing new arrangements with other companies for Cement's Brisbane terminal was purely the relationships that would help propel Chris' career. Chris planned to progress to another company, thought Colin, leaving Colin behind to deal with the problems.

Seizing opportunity, several industries arose around the principle of sustainability. Customers paid Cement's waste recycling business to dispose of their industrial waste in Cement's kilns and elsewhere. (Greg had no objection to me taking an insurance broker to Dandenong to inspect the business until I mentioned, as an aside, that I was looking forward to seeing it. "That's no reason to go," he snapped. Never again did I admit to enjoying anything.)

Cement was pleased to experiment with burning worn rubber tyres in its kilns, until someone calculated that the costs of doing so exceeded the savings from not burning other fuels. Chris decided the company wouldn't burn any more tyres unless the price of other fuels rose or a government gave the company money to do so. (Wanting governments to keep out of our lives doesn't keep businesspeople and everyone else from asking governments for money.)

We espouse environmental sustainability whenever doing so is profitable: selective sustainability. Mountains of useless worn tyres might prove to be our most enduring legacy.

Production of goods requires raw materials, just as farming requires fertile land. In perfect fruition, our economies could be immortal, but in the postmodern West even immortality has to make good business sense.

A business plan for the southern premerger company had reputedly been to minimise all investment and let its manufacturing capacity decline and die. It would then import what it wanted to sell.

Five years after I left Cement, Chris closed and dismantled the company's New South Wales plant almost a century old. Apparently he did so, because it was nearing the age when heritage laws would protect its most interesting, even beautiful, features.

Cement's plant in rural Tasmania was a century old. Near it, a relatively modern single-storey, brick building had been the administrative centre for the southern premerger company. Employees maintained green lawns with bright yellow flowers and a picnic area for lunch around it, but the merger forming Cement made most of those employees redundant. To save costs, Chris wanted employees who remained to take space in the dusty confines of the plant and the brick building demolished.

Demolishing the building would cost money but that cost would be the last, without the running expense. Just leaving the building empty, with electricity disconnected, wouldn't satisfy Chris. "There'll still be costs," he told the executive committee, shaking his head, "whatever they are."

I wondered if he wanted to destroy the building for it being a symbol of the past, in a clear declaration that everything had changed. Employees (including several who'd never worked anywhere else) might've looked back fondly to what their jobs had been.

To me, wilfully destroying a nice, solid building was wasteful, even if there was no cause to maintain it. I'd have preferred he left it alone: dark and still. Were we a people, destroying a popular asset would be self-destructive, but we're individuals. (Were we a people, we wouldn't have contemplated running down our manufacturing capacity to then import.) Chris' self was he and he alone.

I don't know what persuaded Chris to let the building remain. Demolition costs might've been too high, even for him. More likely, he realised its rooms were cleaner places for him to sit when he visited the site.

Adjoining the wood-panelled, old boardroom was a much less interesting meeting room, which was the setting for an irregularly convened meeting of the Cement superannuation policy committee. Wayne decided the committee should spread its meetings around company sites, although we five or so members did nothing at those sites but meet in a room and eat sandwiches.

Uniquely among the meetings in which Wayne and I both sat, he normally had little to say. Wayne sat silently, reading something unrelated to the meeting around him. The rest of us discussed superannuation funding employees' retirement, supporting people's dependants (not an issue for Wayne), and providing life and disability insurance.

Employees normally retired at age sixty-five. "I'll be working when I'm *seventy-five* years old," Wayne nonchalantly remarked, surprising us that he spoke at all. His was a statement without feeling, although he might've intended to mean we needn't dwell upon anyone's retirement because we needn't dwell upon his. On the other hand, he might've just wanted to tell us.

No one responded. The rest of us glanced at each other, before resuming the discussion unperturbed. We planned to retire no older than sixty-five. Without saying so, I imagined retiring sooner.

For as long as I'd known him, my Chinese friend James leapt eagerly through a succession of jobs and commercial ventures, such as a small shop in Chatswood selling stamps and golfing equipment shortly after we finished studying business together. The connection between stamps and golf so obvious to him was never obvious to me, but they were his interests and the shop was a fun place to browse.

"I'll never retire," James told me, sitting on the sofa in the lounge room of our home. "We have no children." His and Irene's childlessness was more likely a matter of chance than of choice, but twenty-four hours in a day can seem a long time, seven days a week. "What else would we do?"

The West was supposedly becoming richer. Yet the brief era when people like Reuben, the Holyman finance director, retired aged fifty-five had passed.

Reuben preceded me as company secretary of TNT Shipping & Development, where Sir Ian Potter was a director and board chairman. Reuben told me Sir Ian's aged eyes often slipped closed during board meetings, but his age and accomplishments were reasons for other directors and Reuben politely to continue their meeting without comment. I wondered why a man so tired was still working (even if only as a public company chairman).

Sir Ian died aged ninety-two, after a long illness. He'd only retired from the finance committee for a science academy the previous year.

Lives, even long lives, needn't necessarily have consequence. Near the tarnished brass plaque of my mother's grave is a tarnished brass plaque marking the grave of a William Kyle. The plaque recorded that he was head of Simms Motor Units, setting the honest example in business. The company, I discovered, ceased to exist more than twenty years before he died.

Few places are more challenging and more inspirational to explore than cemeteries. We do well to imagine what might be said or written of us when we die, if anything. My grave shouldn't refer to anything I write. It certainly shouldn't refer to Cement.

Two hundred years earlier, Thomas Jefferson wanted his grave to describe him being the author of the American Declaration of Independence, author of the Virginia Statute for Religious Freedom, and father of the University of Virginia. At least William Kyle's grave mentioned his wife.

By the time I reached Babcock & Brown in 2007, mortality was just another business opportunity. One of Babcock's more imaginative investments had been in a business buying the life insurance policies of terminally ill people. Depending upon whether the policyholders co-operated and died at optimum times (from the company's point of view), relative to what the actuaries had forecast, then the business might make windfall profits. Conversely, if they were difficult and died at other times, they might diminish the business returns. Payable to their nominated beneficiaries, the policy proceeds were their life's receivables.

Babcock sold the business. The buyer sued Babcock alleging executives knew insurers were refusing to pay on the policies.

The postmodern West applies commercial principles to sustainability of people. Our solitary lives are, of course, worth much more than other solitary lives. (We've no equality about that.) We buy the happiness so life's benefit satisfies its cost. Prolonging our lives might warrant any cost when we're old nearing death, if we still have capacity to spend. Until then, we focus too much on the moment to care so far ahead. Pleasures each day are worth more than pain many years on. Our health is an issue only if it immediately affects us, however much our lifestyles eventually might kill us. The only pain that matters is the pain we feel today.

Through my undergraduate university years, many of us felt the pressure of examinations. I heard of one student the morning of his examination jumping from a university building to his death.

(I tell my children not to fret: to study and learn, but not fret. Examinations create options; that's all. We have options whatever our examination results.)

My wife's brother attended several twenty-first birthday parties. One was memorable not so much for the scores of people who were there, but for the person who wasn't. She'd been a good student, who enrolled in a course after finishing school. The following year, she enrolled in a different course. Her parents would ultimately convene her twenty-first birthday party because, unable to decide what she wanted to do with her life, she'd killed herself.

Studies and work were no longer merely the most important facets of our lives. They'd become our lives.

When a beautiful young actress taking drugs and excessive alcohol fell more than ten metres from the balcony of her apartment and died, a newspaper mourned the waste of her talent. The newspaper presumed there's nothing more to life than the work we do, and nothing more to death than the work we'd have done.

If work is everything, then failure at work is failure at everything. The prestigious private girls' school at which my wife was a teacher claimed to have waiting lists for new students. Fee-paying parents felt special for their daughters being accepted, while the school quietly advertised for more students. One successful pupil was determined to be a published novelist before her twenty-fifth birthday, but wasn't. So, she jumped from a bridge to her death.

Unnatural selection began with the West's rejection of race and collective religion. With economics unfettered, the human condition withers. We concede our days to make what doesn't really matter, letting ourselves expire to earn little bits long dead. We take crazy things too seriously, when the world and being alive are ours to relish.

The most beautiful and bright give up their lives to keep trivialities intact.

We once presumed our time at work to be important, proud of our performance, but nothing changed because of anything we did. Among the few managers I encountered who did cast impressions, too many, particularly at the most senior levels, wreaked only anguish upon employees not so far devolved as they were. I might have, too. Some people might've increased production of mining or manufacturing output, or improved transport or shipping services, but the output and services were already enough. Most of the rest could walk on wet sand without leaving footprints.

Jobs are poor indications of how good, interesting, or important we are. I often talked with the principal cleaner at the building in which Holyman kept its offices. Years later, I smiled with him when we saw each other outside. He made better company than did most directors. The woman replenishing supplies at the eleven Babcock & Brown kitchens made better company than did most employees.

Doctors and nurses save people's lives but only for a while, deferring their deaths. The closest they and midwives get to creating lives is helping parents create them.

Valuing promotions more than parenthood, we might well die old and rich. We might die in the company of our computer terminals or alone while the nurses are in other rooms, watching their television sets or playing with their telephones. The closest networks of our friends might enjoy half a day of compassionate leave to attend a small service for our passing, if they can reschedule their appointments at the office and with their pedicurists. A recruiter might arrange our replacements, or the remaining staff might reconfigure their roles to take up what we'd done. No one need know that we've gone, and no one need know we've been here.

21

Infanticide

I liked Clive, the United Kingdom finance director at Holyman, although the day the company and its joint venture partner launched our English Channel ferry service, he watched the rest of us work. Fred, an accountant, and I had expected to enjoy that Saturday among the celebrants enjoying the festivities, but so unexpectedly great was the demand for duty-free goods, I carried boxes of items for sale from the storeroom. Fred stood behind a counter selling perfumes. Clive thought being finance director was reason for him to stand idly by.

Long beforehand, Clive and I sat conversing in a lounge at the Royal Horseguards Hotel, London. He claimed he and his wife could do more with their lives without children.

"What things?" I asked, before I knew they didn't include carrying boxes or selling perfumes.

"Go to concerts," replied Clive, or something as such.

"Haven't you heard of babysitters?"

He listed more things, all of which I'd done, or could've done if I'd wanted to. With bearing children natural, we don't need a reason to be parents but reason not.

Beyond the trauma of birth, Western men and women share much the same reasons for not wanting to be parents. Our arbiters of fashion, style, and success set their terms without reference to children; self-destructive slaves to other people's thoughts let us all go down.

In 2012, Edith Cowan University psychology lecturer Bronwyn Harman published the results of a survey of three hundred and thirty adults, most of them women. Three quarters of respondents without children were childless by choice.

Sixteen percent thought children would ruin their lifestyle. "They want the ability to go out, work, and travel," said Harman. (Children in the house impinge upon us being the centres of our self-centred worlds; other lives might curtail our choice of hobby.)

Eight percent were concentrating upon their careers. (We think our lives are just ours, and we've so many other people to be.)

The same percentage didn't have children because they thought it "was a bad world to bring children into." (Western individualism can't have looked too good to them.)

Another seven percent reported an active dislike of children. "To the extent where some said they were even annoyed if they had to step out of the way of prams when they came past them."

Two percent chose not to have children because they were concerned about passing on genetic conditions. (That might've been an honourable reason. American television presenter Bill Nye decided not to have children because his family suffered ataxia, although he'd "dodged the genetic bullet.")

A similar percentage believed they couldn't afford to have children. We don't give money to our parents, except for something in return, so can't imagine our children supporting us, ushering money our way when we no longer earn. Feeling financially insecure in spite of all that we have, we let money keep us from parenting.

When a global financial crisis stirred New Zealand in 2008 and 2009, Henderson Medical Centre specialist Dirk Venter in Auckland and other doctors reported a steep rise in men seeking vasectomies. (I don't ever want to feel that financially insecure.) Venter refused men who'd never had children.

Commercial advertising never says so, but my children save me money. They entertain my wife and me for hours without the ticket costs of lesser shows, delighting us more than we'd thought they could. Not wasting time away from our children frees us to enjoy them more. Who could've imagined the day our firstborn children saw the moon in the sky at the back of our home and thought they could touch it, repeatedly leaping high from the edge of the porch?

I've enjoyed parenting more than I imagined I would. I've met people I'd have otherwise not met, seen places I'd have otherwise not seen, and done things I'd have otherwise not done. None of it was a sacrifice, because I'm not just an individual. I've shared in the joys and successes of my wife and children because we're a family.

Our economies could be correct, if we live for the minute instead of the moment, if we live for all our family's lives instead of single instants in just ours. Happiness maximised could include the loves we feel instead of just the things we buy and do. It could encompass the happiness of those we love.

It's become commonplace in the West to say economic prosperity reduces birth rates, without mentioning that no birth rates have reduced more than ours. Unlike other races, we measure success by something other than parenthood, as if the only prosperity were material, individual, and immediate. Most obviously in the Middle East oil emirates, wealthy Arabs see their riches as reasons to bear more children. Poor Africans bear children nevertheless.

Paradoxically, the richest of people are the most conscious of what bearing children might cost; those with the most are the most determined to keep it. If we feel rich, we see children no less than we see everything else in monetary terms; not for us the relationship or mere immortality. If we bear children then it's because the benefits to us outweigh the costs, the amusement outweighs the expense. Our children are leisure items much like any other. They're fashion accessories wheeled out for portraiture, not just by film stars seeing paparazzi nearby.

The rich among us would rather holiday each year in Nice; through my one hurried night there, the Negresco was a glorious hotel. Having acquired more goods and services than we ever can use, we acquire still more. Embroiled in work, we hoard ornaments we have no time to see. Our lives become a glut of almost everything, but children. We think we're pleasing ourselves, whiling away in the garden or lying in the hot, bright solarium, while the wealth and resources that should've made us more fertile leave us barren.

We make our toys more important than us. They're too engrossing.

In any meaningful, collective, lasting sense, we're not prospering at all. If we measured wealth by children as other races do, we'd understand how poor we are. Instead of buying a pocket digital camcorder, personal fulfilment would be raising our people. Instead of buying a new kettle that can also poach eggs, happiness would be seeing our people smile. Wealth lies not in gold or money, but warm flesh and blood. We are our greatest riches. Power lies not in names or technologies, but human beings and bodies. If all I was when I died was monetarily rich, I'd be bitterly dissatisfied.

David and Susan Moore published *Child-Free Zone* in 2000, catering to chosen childlessness. Proudly they promoted barrenness for fools wanting to believe them, presumably for the sake of reward. Holed up in cabins in a forest, dying in anonymity, their aged, trembling hands can clutch the last editions of their book, rotting in the damp. They'll weep and wail for someone to bring them medicine, without anyone hearing. Strangers don't come to see loneliness through the years people die, without being paid to do so.

In her 2007 book *No Kid: Forty Reasons for Not Having a Child*, Frenchwoman Corinne Maier complained her two children prevented her living the life that she wanted. (They must really have felt loved.) Maier was also the author of *Hello Laziness: Why Hard Work Doesn't Pay*, so the selfish life her children supposedly denied her wasn't working (or writing books). Journalist Stephen Lunn suggested it was visiting surrealist art exhibitions.

None of the rules we apply to our dealings with other races, we apply to our thoughts of bearing children of our own. We focus on whatever good we imagine comes from racial and religious diversity, while talking only of the troubles of childbearing.

In 2011, journalist Adele Horin commented upon a report *When Baby Makes Three* from the National Marriage Project at the University of Virginia. The headline to her article could hardly have been more negative: 'And baby makes…trouble.' Yet, the article went onto say that children could make parents happier if those parents were generous to their spouse, had good physical intimacy, shared housework, and were religious.

Elizabeth Marquardt and Bradford Wilcox had carried out the research. They wrote in *Atlantic* magazine that married parents, especially women, were more likely to report their "*life had an important purpose*" than their peers without children.

Eric Hudson, vice president of the Australian Association of Relationship Counsellors, alluded to how much the problems that parents thought they had with children really reflected problems in their lives and in their relationships with each other. "Parents living busy lives can overlook the importance of kindness to each other," he said.

In January 2014, the *Telegraph* newspaper in London reported that childless couples were happier about their marital relationships than those with children, but that was a jaundiced view of the results of a survey of five thousand people published by Open University. The survey showed mothers to be the happiest people in Britain. Childless women were least happy, in spite of their more satisfying marital relationships.

Parents who laugh that their child or children are too many make those children so sad. Those children believe their parents, rather than think poorly of them. Their parents' cruelty becomes theirs when they too lie alone, condemned to die in homes too big for one.

In our postmodern West without respect for our forebears,

parenthood becomes the spectre of being like the people our parents were. Too few of us are bold enough to step back from our childhoods for the sake of our children. We let our relationships with our parents determine whether we even bear children, as if we have no chance to do better. The parents that gave us the present we let determine whether we, and they, have futures. Saucy English actress Barbara Windsor never bore children because her father had rejected her as a child.

Well educated as Heather was, the pretty, cleanly kept American allowed the traumas of her relationship with her mother to keep her childless. "She said we could make the world a better place without having children," her husband Ashley told me, sitting in the lounge room of our friend Phil's home two days after our thirty-year school reunion. I didn't think to ask if Heather meant they would make the world better by not having children, or if there were ways to make the world better other than bearing children. Either way, it was all rather sad. They could've parented children, keeping Heather's mother away.

Instead, Heather's great passion was campaigning for the rights of women to abortions. She made quite the contrast to Ashley's mother, also called Heather, who attended church and bore five children, but that was our preceding generation.

Ashley himself had been ambivalent about becoming a parent. I wondered if the financial pressures upon his parents of so many children in private schools discouraged him from bearing children. (It should only have discouraged him from buying them private school educations.)

At school, all those decades ago, Ashley affixed to his diary a newspaper headline reading 'Keeping the wog at bay.' Wogs were colds or influenza viruses but also slang for Southern European immigrants, before the arrivals of Asians, Pacific Islanders, and Africans made the relatively white South Europeans less of an issue. To recall his diary from our youths made me wonder if becoming minorities in our countries makes white people's futures too insecure for us to be parents.

He'd changed since then. That night in Phil's lounge room, talking about my manuscript that became this book, Ashley told us of his pride in being blind to race and religion when hiring people at work; his section was the most racially diverse of the company for which he worked. Not that he was really so blind, not when American federal and state governments only awarded contracts to develop transport systems to businesses appointing ethnic minority subcontractors.

Those subcontractors needed the benefit of government support. Ashley said they were normally appallingly incompetent.

It's all about money. Ashley confessed his discomfort at having become reluctant to hire women of childbearing age, after an employee's recent pregnancy disrupted the business.

"It's to your credit you're worrying about it," I told him.

"Our business needs people to work extra hours," he explained.

"Every business says that," I replied, although I should have confined my comment to Western businesses. "That's how they rationalise it."

Six or seven years before that evening, Ashley read an early draft of my novel *Swansong of a Childless People*. Far from fearing the collapse of a childless European city, he relished grand homes becoming available. At the time, he and Heather were living in what I'm sure was a fine house in Warrawee, among tall trees and near his childhood home.

If we notice our wide road to ruin, then we're confident little will change until we've taken our opportunities for gain. (The West mightn't care about white people dying, but we're always looking out for real estate.)

More than most of my non-fiction writing, this book (particularly this chapter) became the repository of facts and ideas expunged from that novel: its themes commanded me to think about the aging and dying of people wilfully childless. If the novel's central character sits late in life with a supply of drying pens and crumbling paper, trying to understand why the West ceased bearing children, he'd write something like this book.

Our children don't just teach us how to use and circumvent the most modern technologies and new waves in slang. Rewards richer than all others, we have perpetuity. The lives my wife and I will leave behind aren't just our children and, I trust, grandchildren and even great-grandchildren. They're the children forever that natural and unnatural selections allow. Our children's children so many years yet to be born make our family immortal, for as long as we continue.

The human species is better for all of us. I'm biased, of course.

Infertility is mortality. If we let ourselves grow old without being fathers and mothers, then we've done nothing at all. All our reasons not to bear children, are fearful of bearing children, are furphies, when so few of us remain. Childless lives that people call great are sick jokes upon themselves.

Our last heroines and heroes are women and men who, in spite of every pressure upon them, bear us a future. Each one loving life enough to bring a child onto the earth, meaning to do the best by him or her, saves the world. Whatever else we do or don't do doesn't matter, provided somewhere along our lives' long paths, we become parents, perpetuating our people beyond our deaths. Every other achievement, success, and all else we do is dust across the ground aside our sons and daughters, continuing the glory. What parents do is the most important thing we do, we joyous noblemen and women great merely for doing what's natural.

No blight from our new Western ideologies is greater than the end of our child making. Our impersonal tenets are manifest, but we live too well to see what we've become. Our work and active leisure, items of manufacture and other people's service, conceal the barrenness within us.

Never was the inhumanity of our attitude to children more evident than in the case of Keli Lane, and she gave birth to them. As well as being busy socialising, she wanted to play water polo at the 2000 Olympic Games in Sydney.

Falling pregnant five times between 1992 and 1999 was no reason to disturb her interests or ambition. She terminated the first two pregnancies. Two other babies she secretly carried to term and adopted out in 1995 and 1999, which was far more generous of her time than most of us are. Her fourth pregnancy she also hid from her family, friends, and boyfriend, even after her daughter Tegan was born on the twelfth day of September 1996 at Auburn Hospital (where she was conspicuous as a rare Western baby), but she'd accepted an offer to coach water polo at the prestigious Ravenswood School for Girls a few weeks later.

Almost fifteen years onward, when news services reported her trial, I wondered why she didn't give up Tegan for adoption. If she'd done so, she could have again been a heroine, but perhaps that was too much inconvenience. The West has become indifferent to Western people's lives, including Western children's lives, as is our right being individuals. Two days after giving birth, during the four or five hours between leaving Auburn Hospital and attending a wedding with her boyfriend, Lane murdered her baby.

22

Management with a Human Face

Among my colleagues at TNT and Holyman, early in my working life, there were fathers to numerous children. Ed was father to five daughters. Griff and Graham were fathers to four children each.

In 1996, I became a father. Roly, formerly the managing director at TNT Shipping & Development and by then the deputy chairman of the Holyman board, became a grandfather. Standing by the Holyman reception desk, with the huge Holyman name and logo behind it, Roly talked about how much he enjoyed being a grandfather.

"Is that because you get to give them back?" I asked, expecting him to say what so many Western people said disparagingly of their grandchildren, nieces, and nephews.

"No, no," he said, surprising me. "It's because when you're a parent, you worry," he explained, or words to that effect. "You worry about them getting hurt, about their education. Then you worry about their relationships and getting a job. When you're a grandparent, you don't worry about those things." I expected him to say those problems weren't his, but he didn't. "You know they're going to be all right. You can sit back and enjoy them."

Any sensitivity to the human condition was rare among business leaders with whom I worked, but Roly understood what he was, I was, and each of us could be. Loving parents can't really relax until their children are securely married and parents, too. If a corporation is to be anything worthwhile, it would be a grandparent.

A rare child I saw in a city office building was a baby in a pram at the offices of some particularly dubious financial advisers, during my time at Holyman. I'm not sure if particularly dubious financial advisers were more likely to accept visitors with children, or if parents were a little more trusting. (A father I might've been, but I wasn't trusting of schemes by which investors could claim tax deductions far in excess of their investments by saying they were early payments of interest. Neither, it turned out, was the Australian Taxation Office.) In any

event, I made a point of smiling and saying to the mother how much I
liked seeing a child in a city office building.

Peter (a lawyer of Polish ancestry) worked with me at the second
law firm at which I worked after my admission as a solicitor. Almost
twenty years later, during my last year at Cement Australia, he'd long
left behind his career ambition and pretence of job satisfaction. Instead,
he had a wife, two children, and comfortable home. Three things he
wanted from a job: to be interested in his work, to work with nice
people, and to be paid well. If a job gave him two of those three, he
was content.

The lures vocational guidance counsellors held before us in our
youths, no longer beckoned. (If people capable of doing a job do it
and people incapable of doing a job teach it, or write books about it,
then people incapable of doing any damned job become vocational
guidance counsellors.)

At Cement, I talked about work as far as I and other people needed
to do. When there was no call to do so, I asked about people.

Among the people with whom I conversed was An-janette: a tall,
thin woman I first met at the second finance division conference,
convened at the Palm Meadows Resort behind the Gold Coast in
Queensland. (Her father also worked at the company, at an age by
which most men had retired. I imagine his past work helping
Aborigines paid so little money he needed to keep working.) If I spoke
a little more to An-janette than I spoke to most employees, then it was
because she'd recently become a mother.

Another year or more later, the 'Diversity in Action' article boasting
of Jackie's appointment also boasted of An-janette's return to work
"*part time after giving birth to twins.*" It said An-janette was a BPI analyst,
which presumably meant something to do with business process
improvement. (We have no end of phrases to describe people's jobs
and acronyms to conceal them.) Her job wasn't something I recalled
us discussing. She'd long ago told me she was unsure about whether
to bear more children, until her conversation or conversations with me
about mine, in part, led her to bear another, or two.

It seems we hadn't caught up with each other after her return to
work when, a week before my final day a Cement employee, An-
janette sent me an electronic mail message. "*I understand that you are
leaving Cement…for greener pastures,*" she wrote. "*I wanted to wish you a
fond farewell and to say a special thank you. Whilst this is not something I
would ordinarily share with my work colleagues, I hope you don't find me
too personal by mentioning that my husband and I are considering having*

another child (number 4…). Actually, I am considering it much more then my husband is, although I think I have been persuasive enough for him to give up resisting!

"*My reason for thanking you is that I have always been uplifted by the positive way you speak of your family and your tribe of children… I hope your future is filled with much happiness, Kind regards A-j.*"

Amidst my reply, I wrote: "*As to numbers of children, the more the better. Each one is a life, with hopes and fears, joys and sadness, and I would rather lose every material possession I have than any of mine.*"

"*Beautiful! Uplifting once again,*" she wrote, the day before my final day a Cement employee. "*I do get frustrated when I am given reasons for not having more children such as "you'll need a bigger car…a bigger house…kids are so expensive" as though these material considerations should be the determinants as to whether we bring another human life into this world!*"

With values and character so important to Chris, I really wasn't suited to working at Cement. Other employees were no more suited to being there, but they kept themselves for the most part to themselves: a secret universe, apart from everything they seemed to their managers to be. Nothing An-janette wrote, said, or thought appeared in the *Vision* magazine.

Supporting businesses operated by good family men and women, among the criteria I consider, is discriminatory of me, but legal. My writing might be an act of some insurrection or appear to be a long letter resigning from my corporate career, but in spite of us cherishing our privacy, enough people cited herein will see my observations about them as compliments. Chris and Wayne might tender them to potential employers. Jerry and Sueki probably won't.

Greg accused me of trying to change things at Cement, as if that were wrong. Sure, I tried to introduce social drinks among head office staff on a Friday evening (as I'd done at Otter), and failed. Most of what I did was all most of us did at TNT Shipping & Development and Holyman: my small facets of life I never devolved as far as Greg remained or devolved during his three decades of essentially unchanged employment.

Helping me transport my papers and so forth from the offices to my car through my departure from Cement, my final secretary Naomi surprised me by saying she hoped one day to be a mother. "I didn't think you liked children," I replied. "That's what you told Kaye."

I liked Kaye, the group accountant; we'd laughed together. In my first year at Cement, she'd complimented me that someone in my position could be so approachable that a young accountant like Justin telephoned me about betting on the State Of Origin rugby league games. (I might've distorted Justin's expectations. He would soon leave unhappy at the company's treatment of employees around him. Glen Thomas called him naïve.) Passed over for opportunities I thought she deserved and excluded from meetings to which I thought she could've contributed, Kaye wasn't treated any better than parents were treated at Cement.

Kaye had recently been in Sydney talking with me at Naomi's desk one afternoon, when she mentioned she was glad not to have children. At fifty or so years of age and unlikely to fall pregnant, there'd been no purpose in me trying to persuade her otherwise, but Naomi agreed with her. In the building basement car park where only I could hear her, Naomi explained, "I had to say that."

I told Naomi I hoped her boyfriend would find the good sense to marry her. She smiled, but didn't know if he would. We returned to the offices.

If she wasn't already, Naomi (a law student) became the legal support officer. I couldn't have seen or spoken with her for close to six months when she sent me at my home a Christmas card: a personal card, nothing corporate, wishing the "*Merriest of Christmases to you and your lovely family.*" At the end of the card, she added, "*You are missed!*" Greg would've been comforted to know I achieved no other lasting effect.

Not within Cement anyway. Naomi went onto leave Cement, marry her boyfriend (perhaps not in that order), and become a mother. We kept in touch.

At Babcock & Brown, Gavin clandestinely from his wife bought a colourfully framed photograph she'd admired of the clean sandy beach at which they'd wed. After keeping it hidden by his desk at the offices, he presented it to her for their first wedding anniversary. The gesture revealed romance in him, as nothing else I saw or heard of him did.

Somehow, love and marriage proved not quite enough for him. In response to something I said about my children, Gavin told me (with more fear than joy) that he hoped to have children. "I don't want to end up like Carol."

On Anzac Day 2009, Glen Thomas was again at the Ignite the Flame fair on the St Ives Village Green. This time, the former Cement supply chain general manager and I didn't stride into each other's path. My wife recognised him before I did. With his hair much greyer than I remembered it being and more ruffled than the wintry open air alone made it, he appeared much older than he ought to have appeared.

I don't think Glen saw us among the crowd. With Camilla and their young children, he was a distance away from us, although not so far that my wife couldn't hear them talking. "Now you say goodbye to your father," she told their children. "You won't see him for a few weeks."

I should've approached him, so estranged from everyone, but still didn't know what to say. I knew I shouldn't leave my children too long that day. There'd be another time for Glen and me to talk.

I learnt later he had a fiancée amidst his life getting into some sort of order, but he'd suffered too much. Coincidentally on my forty-seventh birthday and only a few weeks after I saw him, Glen died. He was fifty-four years old.

My wife and I attended his memorial service on the fourth Friday in May at Christ Church, St Ives, not far from the Village Green where last I'd seen him. Nor was it much further from the house where I'd collected him some mornings to drive him with his broken foot to Cement and to which I'd brought him home some evenings.

His smiling face in the photograph in front of the mourners was casual and relaxed, with his shirt open necked and trees behind him. It was much like, but not quite, the photograph of him formerly on the Cement computer site. A company photographer took photographs of each of us executives individually and all of us together five and a half years earlier, through those days we drafted the fledgling company's values: its guiding bloody principles.

(My photographs were somewhere. Wayne had displayed his group photograph in his company office.)

The minister told his one-hour congregation of Glen's guilt for some choices he'd made. I assume they related to his wives and children. "We don't know if Glen was ready to meet his maker," said the minister. "We only know that his maker was ready to meet him."

I couldn't help but wonder if Glen might've been alive that day had he never entered Cement: if an accommodating company could save a man as much as a cruel company could kill him. The answer was unknowable to men mortal like me, not simply because there was no end of similar companies.

No speaker at the service mentioned Cement. The omission made the company unimportant. All companies were unimportant.

Instead, the minister spoke of a man who mightn't have realised how much he'd been a friend. I longed to have said anything to him that

Anzac Day afternoon a month earlier. We so often presume there'll be a next time, until suddenly there was only a last time.

Every day onward, that last time becomes longer ago. Glen's eldest son and daughter gave tempered eulogies, painfully acknowledging their father's flaws, stepping tactfully around two widows left to mourn. Theirs was no beatification, but appreciation. Most profoundly of all, his faithful son thanked Glen for the great gift he'd given him: five brothers and sisters.

Most of the scores of people who attended the service were friends of his children. My wife knew Glen's youngest daughters in her guide troop. I recognised only Camilla. All I knew to say to her afterwards was, "I'm so sorry."

Without other immortality, our only future is the future our children make. Those six children gave Glen life and might yet give him immortality.

Wayne, wherever he was in the world, and other childless executives and caravan park dwellers had no such immortality. Sometime thereafter, I pitied them, as I imagine few people did.

When I told my insurance friend Colin S in 2011 that I'd attended a lawyers' reunion marking twenty-five years since our admission to the Supreme Court, he assumed we'd all been big-noting our careers. He was wrong. Nobody did. At the Union, University, and Schools Club that Friday night, we talked of families and people poor without them.

I told one fellow attendee sitting beside me at dinner, otherwise a stranger to me, that I felt no greater pride than the pride I'd felt a day I stood outside my eldest boys' bedroom door and thought about the family home my wife and I had made. He raised his hand much as that employment lawyer and Wayne had done that night at the Rag & Famish Hotel after Gary was dismissed. I slapped my hand against his: high five! He thought ours was the first generation to think work mattered more than families, or was that the other way around?

And Wayne? He married, fathered two sons, and began working less.

Long after her tumultuous separation and divorce and soon after her widowed father died, pregnancy and motherhood mellowed Carolyn (an only child) at Golden Cross Resources Limited; she told us not to ask who the baby's father was. By then weary of his fellow directors about to dismiss him (and me), Kim couldn't have been more supportive to her.

In spite of Kim telling the woman fulfilling Carolyn's role during her six weeks' maternity leave that she would be paid the same money as Carolyn, Carl paid June the lesser amount he thought she should be paid. Kim overruled him.

The Wednesday a week before Christmas 2014, the Chinese directors and a West Australian director escorted Kim and me from the offices. I'd worked there six years, Kim nearly nine. The company still hasn't mined anything.

More telling than regulation is inspiration. If our epitaphs are that we're grandparents, we'll lie inside the soil more content than anyone with causes or career.

If Roly's words to me long ago somehow facilitated my wife and me parenting more children, then they were the most important words he ever spoke: important to my family and me, at any rate. If anyone mothered or fathered a child because of anything I said or did, then that child would be the greatest achievement of my legal and corporate career. It mightn't seem very much, but none of our colleagues achieved anything more.

Bibliography

Articles

Adami, Christoph and Arend Hintze, 'Evolutionary instability of zero-determinant strategies demonstrates that winning is not everything,' *Nature Communications*, Volume 4, 1 August 2013. Melissa Hogenboom, 'Selfish traits not favoured by evolution, study shows,' *BBC News Science & Environment*, 2 August 2013.

Arlington, Kim, 'No time for five babies: Keli Lane accused,' *The Sydney Morning Herald* newspaper, 10 August 2010.

Bingham, John, 'Happier relationships for couples without children' and 'How mothers are the happiest people in Britain – and how a cup of tea is a bigger turn-on than sex,' *The Telegraph* newspaper, 12 January 2014.

Chasmar, Jessica, 'NYC school cuts popular gifted program over lack of diversity: report,' *New York Daily News*, *Washington Times* newspaper, 30 January 2014.

Clarke, Hannah, 'Do Parents Make Better Managers?' *Forbes* magazine, 27 February 2007, published as 'Mums & dads best managers,' *News Limited Network*, 16 August 2007.

Crabtree, Gerald, 'Our fragile intellect, Parts I and II,' *Trends in Genetics*, Volume 29, Number 1, January 2013. Mike Barrett, 'Leading Geneticist: Human Intelligence is Slowly Declining,' *Natural Society*, 17 February 2013.

Duffin, Claire, 'Fire service is accused of discrimination amid claims it has made entry tests harder for white men to pass than women and ethnic minorities,' *The Daily Mail* newspaper, 28 January 2019.

Durante, Kristina and others, 'Sex Ratio and Women's Career Choice: Does a Scarcity of Men Lead Women to Choose Briefcase Over Baby?' *Journal of Personality and Social Psychology*, 2 April 2012. Christine Hsu, 'Scarcity of Men Drives Women's Career Aspirations, Especially True for Less Desirable Women,' *Medical Daily*, 17 April 2012.

Hope, Lynsey, 'I don't really need a wheelchair... but I would just love to be disabled,' *The Sun* newspaper, 16 July 2013.

Horin, Adele, 'And baby makes ... trouble,' *The Sydney Morning Herald* newspaper, 17 December 2011.

Lynch, Jared, 'Work–life balance? Take condoms, says Southern Cross Austereo radio boss,' *The Sydney Morning Herald* newspaper, 5 March 2015.

Macrae, Fiona, 'Abortions are safer for pregnant women than having a baby, new advice claims,' *The Mail on Sunday* newspaper, 27 February 2011.

McKie, Robin, 'Is Human Evolution Finally Over?' *The Observer* newspaper, 3 February 2002.

Moor, Keith, 'Foreign students 'cheating or receiving special treatment to get degrees',' *Herald Sun* newspaper, 10 June 2010.

O'Brien, Susie, 'Australian couples opting for one child only,' *Herald Sun* newspaper, 4 June 2008, quoting Nick Parr's study published in the *Journal of Population Research*.

Orr, Aleisha, 'Three quarters of those without children are so 'by choice',' *WA Today*, 5 September 2012.

Palan, Simon, 'Survey finds many Australian employers value men over women, prefer workers without children,' *Australian Broadcasting Corporation News*, 21 July 2013.

Petersen, Michael and others, 'The Ancestral Logic of Politics: Upper-Body Strength Regulates Men's Assertion of Self-Interest Over Economic Redistribution,' *Psychological Science* journal, Volume 24, Number 7, July 2013, first published 13 May 2013. Daily Mail reporter, 'Men who are physically strong are more likely to have right wing political views,' *Daily Mail* newspaper, 16 May 2013.

Rivas, Alexis, 'San Diego Unified School District Changes Grading System to 'Combat Racism',' *NBC News San Diego*, 15 October 2020.

Spriggs, Merle, 'Lesbian couple create a child who is deaf like them,' *Journal of Medical Ethics*, Volume 28, Issue 5, 2002.

Uncredited, ''Disruptive' Non Smokers Fired,' *Reuters* news service published at *News Limited Network*, 10 January 2008.

Uncredited, 'India's Baby Farm,' *Sun-Herald* newspaper, 6 January 2008.

Uncredited, ''Lookism' is the New Racism,' *Marie Claire* magazine published at *Yahoo! News*, 5 September 2011, quoting Daniel Hamermesh.

Uncredited, 'Report on the Dayton Police Department,' *ABC Dayton News*, 11 March 2011.

Uncredited correspondents in Auckland, 'More New Zealand men get the snip as recession hits,' *Australian Associated Press* news service, 15 May 2009.

Weiss, Tara, 'How Open Is Your Office?' 14 August 2007, *Forbes* magazine, confirming that when mental issues don't obviously harm productivity or sales, people accept them.

Books and Letters

Appleton, Nicole, born 1974, and Natalie, born 1973, *Together*. Uncredited, 'Why I aborted Robbie's baby,' *The Sydney Morning Herald* newspaper, 10 October 2002. London Records denied their allegation.

Collins, James (Jim), born 1958, *Good to Great* (2001).

Darwin, Charles, 1809-1882, *On the Origin of Species* (1859).

Darwin, Charles, 1809-1882, *The Descent of Man, and Selection in Relation to Sex* (1871).

Darwin, Charles, 1809-1882, *The Variation of Animals and Plants under Domestication* (1868), especially page 6.

dei Machiavelli, Niccolò di Bernardo, 1469-1527, *The Prince* (1513). Concerned with political machinations, the book's essential thesis has been, perhaps unfairly, widely interpreted as being that the end justifies the means.

Keneally, Thomas, born 1935, *Schindler's Ark*, known also as *Schindler's List*, (1982).

Maier, Corinne, *No Kid: Forty Reasons For Not Having a Child* (2007), and *Hello Laziness: Why Hard Work Doesn't Pay* (2005). Stephen Lunn, 'No Blokes or Babies on the Road,' *The Australian* newspaper, 16 July 2007.

Moore, David and Susan Moore, *Child-Free Zone* (2000). Daryl Passmore, 'Adults only – Queensland's growing market for kids-free zones,' *The Sunday Mail* newspaper, 28 April 2002.

Spencer, Herbert, 1820-1903, *Principles of Biology* (1864), especially Volume 1, page 444.

Essays

Gould, Stephen Jay, 'Darwin's Untimely Burial' (1976), published in Michael Ruse, editor, *Philosophy of Biology* (1998), Prometheus Books. It interpreted Charles Darwin's view of survival of the fittest in terms of suitability to the immediate environment more than physical ability.

Films

Enron: The Smartest Guys in the Room (2005), a documentary.
Incredibles, The (2004).
Wayne's World (1992).

Television Programmes

Big Brother (2001-2008), Australian Ten Network copied, as so many shows are, from elsewhere.
Bill Nye: Science Guy (2017), Public Broadcasting Service.

About the Author

Simon Lennon has lived, worked, and travelled throughout America, Europe, Australasia, Asia, and the South Pacific, seeing how similar European peoples are to each other (wherever we live) and how different we of the West are to everyone else. He has university bachelor's degrees in science and law and university master's degrees in commerce and business. He is married with six children.

His collection *The West* comprises the following fifteen non-fiction books.

The Unnatural West
The Tribeless West
The Homeless West
The Vanishing West

Individualism
Western Individualism
The End of Natural Selection
The Need for Nations

Identity
People's Identity
Of Whom We're Born
Biological Us

Nationalism
A Land to Belong
The Failure of Multiculturalism

Cultures
Reclaiming Western Cultures
Christendom Lost
Aiding Islam

He is also the author of another non-fiction book, two short story collections, and five novels.